© Text: Heike Geissler; Spector Books, Leipzig, 2014.
Original edition published in German in the Volte series, volume 2, edited by Jörn Dege and Mathias Zeiske for Spector Books, 2014.
English edition published by agreement with Spector Books and Heike Geissler, Leipzig, Germany.
This edition © Semiotext(e) 2018

Published by Semiotext(e)
PO BOX 629, South Pasadena, CA 91031
www.semiotexte.com

Special thanks to Robert Dewhurst, and Kevin Vennemann.

Cover: Gerhard Richter, *Betty* (1988), oil on canvas, 102 × 72 cm.
© Gerhard Richter 2018 (0079)

Design: Hedi El Kholti
ISBN: 978-1-63590-036-1

Distributed by the MIT Press, Cambridge, MA, and London, England.

Heike Geissler

Seasonal Associate

Translated by Katy Derbyshire

Afterword by Kevin Vennemann

semiotext(e)

Contents

Five

You show off with chocolates you can't afford. I consider what actually works. Together, we fall over backwards. And aside from that, it's Monday.

Six

For a while, you know your way around the job. But then you have a cubi-tote problem. And that's a real and lasting big deal.

Seven

You're sick and worried the illness might have disappeared overnight. The doctor's job might not be any better than yours. And it's worth sticking out a leg to trip up the working world.

Eight

You have dismissive armies inside you. But at least it's snowing, and you're back to health. Aside from that: books! And a brief crush adds bonus power on the job.

Nine

It'll soon be Christmas so it's time to act. My boyfriend gets more mail from Amazon. You work the turbo shift and you've had enough.

Ten

You're nearly through. First, though, you want to talk about the weather. Your new best friend is a soccer hooligan, and taped choirs don't count.

Eleven

Have you actually taken action now? You've got a whole lot done, but you still have little idea of freedom. And Amazon wants to employ you again.

"Dear Ms...,

Thank you for your interest in a position as a Seasonal Associate at Amazon Distribution GmbH.

We are pleased to invite you to the next Selection Day on our premises this coming Wednesday at 1 p.m. This day gives you an opportunity to find out about the various positions at Amazon. You can then take a practical selection test in the working area of your preference.

We have vacancies in the following areas:

Inbound stock: standing activity, working with PC

Stock storage: walking activity, working with hand scanner

Order fulfillment: walking activity, working with hand scanner

Packaging: standing activity, packaging items, working with scanner

Should you be unable to attend on this date, please contact us to arrange a new appointment.

Our address is:

Amazon Distribution GmbH

Amazonstrasse

Leipzig

Please note that we unfortunately cannot reimburse travel expenses for the appointment. We look forward to meeting you!

With best regards,

Your Human Resources Department"

One

Is all this a matter of life and death? I'll say no for the moment and come back to the question later. At that point, I'll say: Not directly, but in a way yes. It's a matter of how far death is allowed into our lives. Or the fatal, that which kills us. To be precise: compared to that which kills us, death is nothing but an innocent waif. Or: death, compared to that which kills us, is a gentleman with good manners and a shy look in his eye.

From now on, that which kills us is your constant companion; that much I can say. But first of all we'll set out, because you have a job interview. You set out and I'll accompany you and tell you what it's all like and what's happening to you. From now on, you are me. That means you're female; please don't forget that because it's important in places. You're a writer and a translator, and at this point in life you have two sons and a partner who suits you well, something you're usually aware of. Another important thing, which you rarely think about but which has to be said: You're German, but the country you were born in no longer exists.

Your boyfriend wished you luck before you left home and told you yet again that you don't have to do this. But that's not true; you do have to do it, you have to take the first job that comes up, to get some money in the bank.

Your job interview isn't called a job interview, so you haven't thought up anything to say or put on any special clothes. You're wearing jeans and a sweater; we're not talking about a career move here. You leave the house, possibly nervous because you want the job; you haven't got any money and you refuse to claim welfare for certain reasons that I'll explain later. You do get child benefits for the two boys; you can pay your bills, but unfortunately they usually don't get paid on time. An aggravating factor is that you're not good at writing invoices either; you tend to put them on the back burner. That back burner is a long way back, about a mile. You never send out payment reminders either. You think people won't give you any more work if you do. You are now, if you weren't already, a delicate soul. You're very sensitive—you have that in writing—but don't worry too much about it. People shouldn't hold your sensitivity against you; from now on you're welcome to regard your sensitivity as a form of potential. Your vulnerability harbors all kinds of options. As I said: you're sensitive and you'll stay that way—and we'll be coming back to that, too.

Possibly, even this trip to Amazon, which you're not yet sure will bring success—that is, a short-term employment contract—might seem to you like the beginning or the evidence of a slide down the social ladder. You'll try over and over to view it differently, but even from the start, the experience forces you to your knees and down a social stratum, and that's the way it will stay. Yes, you'll start to see strata in society, if you don't already. You'll see the strata before your eyes as clearly as geologists see the structure of the ground where they've dug a deep pit. When you think about it, you sometimes come to the conclusion that the term "downward social mobility" is only a makeshift description for something that is in fact closer to a solidified lack of options and farsightedness. So this is how it will be: You'll get the job and you'll be pleased to have gotten it, and then you'll be tired, you'll hardly keep your eyes open every day. You won't have enough energy for anything pleasurable, or for anything at all, and you'll know a great deal more about your life and the lives of your parents and all those who have bosses. You don't normally have a boss. You'll soon know something about life that you didn't know before, and it won't just have to do with work, but also with the fact that you're getting older, that two children cry after you every morning, that you don't want to go to work, and that something about this job and many other kinds of jobs is essentially rotten.

You'll spend a lot of time thinking about what work is, why work ought not to be imposed on anyone. You'll misunderstand things and muddle things up and your sensitivity will be processed and challenged by the very first instance of the fatal, so it will take you a while to find out what's really troubling you, and to realize that your trouble and suffering are by no means specific to you, but astonishingly generic. Yes, you are generic; I intend to regard you as generic and introduce you to your most generic traits. But the specific ones come first.

At any rate, it's almost impossible not to be forced to your knees and into defiance by this job you're about to have.

You take the number 3 tram to Sommerfeld. The carriage fills up until the station; most people get off there and no one gets on. You assume that all those still on the tram are going to the group interview at Amazon, like you. You look at your note: tram to Teslastraße/Heiterblick, then Amazonstraße.

Pale winter sun. You're now on your way to attempt to participate in the company's pre-Christmas rush. But it could equally be Easter or any other surge in orders coupled to a particular season or holiday that might yield a job for you here. For the time being, though, it's winter, Christmas is not far off, and it'll soon be very cold. The tram heads further and further out of the city center; many of the buildings lining the tracks are empty. After a while, as you approach the city's functional regions, grassy areas and industrial plots prevail: gas stations, car rentals, crane rentals, brothels, vacant office complexes, prefabricated housing projects at some distance from the street. You're nervous; it hasn't died down yet. You cast about for an appropriate mental position, a way of thinking that prevents the thought that no one must see you on this trip out of town. You're sitting on the tram on your way to the test day because you're interested in the company. You're a book person and you're perfectly within your rights to be interested in the company for research purposes. You'll learn to say, however, that you just need the money, that you have this job but you're still a writer and translator. Lots of things are possible. At some point you'll find it easy to cast all your strange ideals of careers and life and success overboard, to say that you have this job, your actual job, and another one on the side. That's when you'll know it's not all your fault, and that that construction worker carrying four wooden beams so heavy they bent his legs into an O, the one my younger son and I watched on the job, was wrong when he said to my son: You pay attention in school so you don't have to do a job like this later on.

You'll be constantly thinking about what ideas everyone has about making a living, why it sometimes feels like failure when you can't live off your actual job. You'll surprise even yourself when you abandon all heroic narratives of success, ideas of getting somewhere with hard work, and instead begin to praise idleness and oppose the eternal commandment of competition and growth. You'll nevertheless utter the occasional sentence that prompts your boyfriend to say you're the only neoliberal left-winger he knows. You'll think about that. There's always something for you to think about. As trite as it sounds, that needs to be said.

You're the only person to get off the tram at Amazon's stop and you immediately know what a global corporation looks like. It can't be missed, but it could be improved. The dispatch hall is built gray and low, parallel to the street; it's huge but discreet. It appears docile, like a tamed giant or a prisoner on parole trying hard neither to do anything criminal nor to look like he might. There's a banner on the fence surrounding the building, announcing job vacancies. Your boyfriend told you not to worry about failing the interview, they're bound to take you. But you're not the kind of person who doesn't think about things, although of course the question is whether worries are even thoughts at all, and not reflexes.

You stand outside the turnstile to the corporate premises and press the visitors' bell. You try to get your bearings quickly; you don't want to get in anyone's way. You follow the instructions written on a sign, directing you to look into the camera above you as you ring the bell and wait. The turnstile doesn't move. You ring three times while staring into the camera, not knowing if you have to trigger the opening mechanism with your eyes or why you need to look into the camera at all, something you don't seem to be able to manage anyway. It doesn't occur to you that your eyes might merely be filling up a screen placed among many other screens at the security counter in the lobby, ignored and unimportant. A green light flashes and you push against the revolving gate, but the turnstile won't turn. In the end, an employee presses his ID card past you to the sensor from the right, pushes against the revolving gate, which immediately begins to revolve, and sends you through with a hearty "In you go."

Ahead of you is a concrete tower, which you enter because it seems obvious and because the man who let you in did the same. The tower is yellow and, as you'll soon learn, is called Banana Tower because of its color. It's the staircase to a metallic bridge that leads in turn to the hall. A laminated photo of a male hand gripping the handrail is stuck to one wall, alongside it the instruction *Use the handrail!* You don't use the handrail, you demonstratively refuse to use it, and that may be rather petty of you but it shows what kind of person you are: you don't like taking orders, but people are welcome to ask you nicely.

I'm thinking of a photo of a price list from a café in Nice that was all over the Internet. The sign explains how the price of a coffee is related to the way it's ordered. If you say "One coffee," you pay seven euros, "One coffee, please" costs you €4.25; and if you say "Hi there, can I get a coffee, please?" the coffee will only cost you €1.40. Sadly, it's not as though *your* hourly wage or your fees go up when people are rude to you, put you under pressure, or treat you disrespectfully.

When you spot the handrail photo on the next level of the tower, you put your hands in your pockets and grace the surveillance cameras in the corners of the ceiling with a cool stare. You still have the time and the energy for that kind of thing.

The staircase tower releases you on the third level. The bridge to the hall entrance clatters beneath your footsteps. Below, trucks are parked at the docks. The docks are temporary extensions of the hall; they look like they're held on by suction. A DHL truck undocks and drives off. You stumble over a floor mat.

And there you stand, now on pale floor tiles. On your right are people waiting on gray chairs, sitting like at a doctor's office, a doctor for those left over, a doctor for the distressed who don't make any great effort to lean away from the worn, greasy wall; they're all going to die anyway. You're one of them now, you see, even though you see it differently and will say all sorts of things to emphasize that there's a distance between you and the other employees and especially between you and the company—but that's not true. You're now in the mouth of the company (in its jaws?) and are being predigested before you're allowed to enter the rest of the digestive tract.

So you sit. From your right comes the stench of unwashed laundry or of laundry hung out to dry in an unaired room, stinky socks. You sit on the last free chair and breathe through your mouth; you'd actually thought you'd have an appointment of your own. You are one woman among many, but if you happened to be a man, you'd be one man among many as well. You'd be sitting there, just like I sat there and just like you're now sitting there as me. So you sit and you look around. Opposite you is a table made of a door on trestles, and this door, which instantly appears incomprehensible, will remain incomprehensible to you. It's a symbol of stinginess and is intended to represent Jeff Bezos's first desk and thus the beginnings of this company, this very successful global corporation. It's obvious that some other symbol could have been chosen, because there's always some other symbol, but it wasn't chosen. You see signs of minor or more major neglect: the dust on the leaves of the plant opposite you, the door that doesn't quite close, the gray patina on the wall above the chairs where the heads and shoulders of many waiting patients have rested and made their mark. The employees at the reception desk watch the images provided by the surveillance cameras half-heartedly or not at all. Behind the reception area, a glass wall enables a clear view inside the hall. Chunky lamps dangle from the ceiling on long cables. A modest light falls through the windows in the roof. It seems restrained beside the huge daylight lamps. From your seat, no employees are visible in the hall, only the empty space above them.

It's easy for you to tell, incidentally, who belongs here and who doesn't. The ones who belong walk the tiles with a relaxed but purposeful stride and don't look around. Most of them wear jeans, hems frayed at the back. Thousands of tiny denim fringes polish the path behind the ones who belong. One of those who belong, a young man with a clipboard in hand and a long key chain, positions himself in front of all the people waiting. He says: Anyone who doesn't know yet what area they want to work in should watch the informational videos in the cafeteria first.

You're curious; you want to see as much as possible but you need these instructions in order to get up from your seat. The cafeteria is large with a view of the parking lot, the tramway tracks, the hill and the field on the other side of the road. A handful of workers are eating lunch. Wearing orange protective vests, they cast brief glances at the people who enter. They say hello to each other, people reply, and then you move toward the TV screens attached to the ceiling, your head leaning back as you stand and watch, one among many.

The film shows how a stock delivery reaches Amazon. A forklift operator drives a huge box to a young employee. She smiles, opens the box, and unpacks it. She scans the barcode on the items, puts them in yellow crates, and pushes the crates onto a conveyor belt. A cuddly elk pokes its head over the edge of a yellow crate, peeking into the world of work as if peeking out of a child's bag packed for a vacation. The elk is the leitmotif of the introduction. It reaches the warehouse in its crate and is then removed from the crate by an employee. Once again, the barcode is scanned, and the elk is placed on a shelf. You have to be a good walker, says the employee in the film. He walks almost ten kilometers a day, he tells you; it saves him from joining a gym. Another employee takes the elk off the shelf, scans the barcode, and packs it in a yellow crate. Again, the elk peeks over the edge of the crate as it travels via transport belt to the packaging station and is finally put in a cardboard box to be sent to a customer.

You think: This is a game everyone's playing. And of course that's what it is—it's a game, a parlor game, and you don't like parlor games, you never have. You're not so familiar, this much can be said, with situations where everyone plays different roles, performs multiple functions. You prefer dealing with people who are what they do. A few years ago you were asked whether what you're looking for is authenticity. The question came from a slightly confused journalist, and you answered yes. Let me tell you, there's nothing wrong with it, simply nothing wrong with authenticity, but if it helps I can also call it *consistency*.

Now, at any rate, you're standing in a line; you don't like standing in line either, but then who does? And aside from that, from now on it will be unavoidable. You're supposed to tell the employee sitting behind a desk at the end of the line what area you want to work in. The employee has all sorts of white sheets of paper and is holding a scratched ballpoint pen. Things are small and handwritten and improvised even in a global corporation. It's your turn and you tell the woman your name. She stands up and yells past you: How am I supposed to work when everyone speaks so quietly I have to ask them three times over? So you speak up a little. You feel as though you're giving away a secret. Two girls snigger behind you; they look entirely young and youthful. Only a few weeks ago, it felt like you were about as young as they are. The two of them laugh more and more, but of course it's only a matter of time before they see the serious side.

What you now know is, for example, that you're surrounded by people who are simply looking for a job, who don't care where they work. There are those who could find other work, who are here by chance or lack of imagination, not by necessity. There are those who have other options or could have them, except that something's going wrong right now. There are those who seem to have other options, just that those options are no better either. And there are those whose other options are worse. Then there are those who seem to assume they had the option of getting a job here but don't actually have that option. All the applicants can be divided into those sent by the employment office and those not sent by the employment office; the latter is a very small group.

Yes, you still have time to let your mind and your eyes wander. You already know plenty about the company, about the sort of work that awaits you here; presumably, you know it all. But for the moment this is still an excursion, an adventure; you're taking mental notes. It's all fascinating. You're not actually here to write about it but you have nothing against experiences and insights into companies you otherwise only encounter through the interface of the Internet.

Everything takes a while; they're very greedy with your time here. They aren't actually keeping an eye on your time. You're at their disposal from the very beginning. You're an item on a list. You're now sitting on a folding bench in a cold white room, waiting for the practical selection test among other trial workers. You're nervous and afraid of messing up. You don't want this job but you're sensible and you have kids who want things every half hour, and your boyfriend wants things occasionally, and you want things of your own as well, although you hardly ever want anything and you usually pretend you need the things you want. You simply need money regardless of the time of year, you're just like anyone else in that respect, and, as you'd like, this can be a comforting truth or a starting point for trying a different way at some point, and not considering the truth incontrovertible.

To your right is a section of room partitioned off by screens providing information on health and safety at work. You see a photo of a swollen thumb blown up to A4 size; it must have been bleeding shortly before the picture was taken, as suggested by a scab along the nail bed and a thin trace of blood toward the fingertip. You turn away, slightly nauseated and unable to get the image of the thumb out of your mind. When a person's sensitive they're sensitive in all areas, something's always upsetting them, and you'll soon notice how something's always coming along that you don't expect and how that's hard to deal with for a delicate soul like you, someone more suited for happiness than unhappiness. Whereby it has to be said right away that no one is suited for unhappiness, yet this fact doesn't get enough recognition, however unbelievable that seems.

Behind you is a man in a thick woolen coat. He's in his early fifties and comes across as though he's just taken a tour around his expansive estate, as though he's just checking up on things here. A boss type of person. You, incidentally, are not a boss type of person, but you've probably guessed that already.

The room is a well-prepared stage that presents the various sections of the company.

At the end of the room where they've recreated a packaging station, a thin older man is laboring over packaging material. Beneath the eyes of the tester—a man a head taller than anyone else with a jaunty paunch and a slightly smug look on his face, the look of a man who doesn't belong and finds everything ridiculously easy, a look that occasionally drifts to the stopwatch in his hand—the trial worker pulls out packaging, set after set, from beside the table and considers which would be best for a DVD. He spreads out the various precut brown cardboard sheets and envelopes in front of him, places the DVD on them to test for size, and finally chooses one cardboard sheet. He examines the DVD in his hands from all sides and misfolds a box so worn by many trial workers' folding that it almost folds itself into shape, the box springing open again the instant he puts the DVD inside it.

You can tell this man has never removed a product from a cardboard envelope and then refolded the packaging as efficiently as possible so as to save space in the trash or keep it for something he wants to send at a later date. You'd like to show the man how to go about it. It would be nothing, easy as pie. The trial worker removes the DVD from the packaging. Stop, calls the tester. Stop, he repeats, as the trial worker puts the DVD back in the box. Your time's up. The tester takes the package and shakes it. Is it supposed to sound like that? he asks. Are you supposed to hear it rattling? He waits. As no answer is forthcoming, he leaves the question unanswered and sends the man to the folding bench, where he's to wait until Human Resources calls him. The tester takes notes. The trial worker sits mutely; you can't tell whether he still has his hopes up. You'd like to know what his motivation is. You always assume people need something, some kind of motivation—a goal, a wish, a clear idea of where they're heading. You're not the kind of person who gets up in the morning and attaches yourself to a day as something balanced, inconspicuous, something that easily pushes you into sleep at night. But no one's like that, although you might get the wrong impression here.

You're shivering and sweating at the same time on the bench. Time's flying; you'll have to pick up your children soon, but you don't want to make a fuss yet. As if for your entertainment, the most beautiful and elegant of trial presentations begins in front of two shelves full of books, CDs, and DVDs. A young woman lifts yellow crates from one pallet onto another empty one beside it. She doesn't bend her back as she does it, holding herself as straight as a rod; she performs all her work calmly, following a well-practiced choreography. This dance, this piling dance, which then becomes a box-counting dance and segues into a locating dance for various products on the sample shelves, is masterfully accurate and ends with lackluster succinctness. You expect a speech at the end, a jump, a banner unfurled to reveal something eye-opening; you expect *something*. The woman, the dancer, goes out to the corridor and eats a granola bar.

When your name is called you walk through a stream of warm air coming down from the ceiling. You say a friendly hello to the tester, as is your habit, and this is not actually worth mentioning but, anticipating what's to come, one could say that circumstances make it worth mentioning: If it were less important to you to say a friendly hello and get a hello back, you'd find a lot of things easier here at the company. But it won't be as linear as that and anyway, there's only a grain of truth to that. The tester hands you a sheet of paper and tells you to read it. It's printed with instructions for the correct lifting and setting down of crates to avoid back damage. You get the impression you'll be given more time to read than to try out. You feel like laughing. You're tempted to hold up the sheet of paper and ask: Seriously? You consider making a suggestion to correct all the spelling mistakes in the short text. But you simply start your trial. Demonstratively, you lift the crates in line with the rules. You bend your knees, squat down, and stand up again without bending your back unduly. Next to you, the thin older trial worker gets a second chance. He's so clumsy you can hardly bear to watch. You don't want to be better than him and certainly not faster. But in comparison to him, you move the crates like a big strong man who could toss anyone in the room here straight up in the air.

Once all the crates are piled you go to the PC station. You're supposed to transfer data from a column on the left into a column on the right. The left column contains typographical mistakes and peculiarities, which are supposed to appear exactly the same way in the right column, without corrections. Later you'll ask yourself why you didn't simply copy-and-paste the information. You retype everything meticulously and start running out of time, the most difficult thing being having to lean over at this normal-height desk without a chair, which makes you nervous.

The other trial worker is allowed to sit down again. You continue to the packaging station. You pack dispatches and hold products in your hands, a game you're familiar with. You're the daughter of a former postmistress, you see, and you spent childhood afternoons or feverish days half-playing, half-helping at your mother's desk or between the shelves behind the parcel counter, packing play parcels, storing play parcels, locating real parcels on the shelves and lugging them to the counter. And you're a customer of the company that now makes you wait on the folding bench yet again.

If you get this job you want to refill your account, which has reached its credit limit, and change banks. That's your dream. You would leave your current bank, which you feel always withholds money when things aren't going well for it, the bank.

At the same time, a searing sense of worry creeps over you and informs you that if they don't take you here and now, you'll only get a job somewhere else that pays even less. If they don't take you now, maybe no one will. You instantly grow ancient and wooden, as though you've crawled out of a dark coal mine. You've completely forgotten that you have a profession and are only here to alleviate momentary poverty. Something inside you is essentially unsettled and will never calm down again, even though you do get the job. From this point on, you are beside yourself with worry.

Two

So now you have a job. That makes you feel much calmer. You calculate over and over how much money you'll earn as a seasonal associate. You work out that the sum you can expect is approximately equal to your overdraft. So you assume you'll soon be able to balance your account and then change banks. Really, you want to get away from your bank; I said that already, and incidentally I still want to get away from that bank too but I haven't managed to yet. I'm like you in that respect, which is of course because here, you—at least to a large extent and only in your imagination, you know—are me. You're no good with money; you often think of what Gertrude Stein wrote: "Everybody now just must make up their mind. Is money money or isn't money money. Everybody who earns it and spends it every day in order to live knows that money is money, anybody who votes it to be gathered in as taxes knows money is not money."

"I remember," wrote Stein, "when my nephew was a little boy he was out walking somewhere and he saw a lot of horses; he came home and he said, oh papa, I have just seen a million horses. A million, said his father, well anyway, said my nephew, I saw three. That came to be what we all used to say when anyone used numbers that they could not count well anyway a million or three. That is the whole point. When you earn money and spend money everyday anybody can know the difference between a million and three. But when you vote money away there really is not any difference between a million and three. And so everybody has to make up their mind is money money for everybody or is it not."

That's what you think of, but it doesn't help much. If someone were to ask you what has to be paid with your money, you'd gaze into a dark crevasse. Your money is very similar to the aforementioned money administered by congresses and presidents, but by now you do try to be more precise and transform the numbers on your screen illustrating the goings-on in your bank account into individual notes and coins. That only works sometimes. You forget what money is. Presumably, the money doesn't remember either what it actually is. At any rate, in the thrill of anticipation you forget all the expenses you have every month and imagine the expected wage payment as a jigsaw piece, a jigsaw piece the size of a boulder, which fits precisely into the enormous gap in your bank account— and then the account would be finished, done, and you could admire it like a completely finished fifteen hundred-piece puzzle. You might not like the motif that much but you can choose another jigsaw, an account with money in it, or simply turn your mind to other things. Sometimes, at least, you want to write invoices for activities for which people don't write invoices. Sometimes you just want to invoice everything and never stop. We'll come back to this, because the end of work—for example, the seasonal work you're about to perform on a daily basis—is not as clear as it seems. That end is, or so it will appear to you, nonexistent. Work simply alters its own physical state, going from a solid to a gas and entering your body through your nose after the actual end of the work, circulating inside you.

So now you're on your way to a training day at Amazon which you won't be paid for taking part in. Of course you ought to be paid for taking part in the training day. There's a quiet complaint to be heard inside you as you approach the company premises, but there's no one there to listen to you, or anyone like you, complain that a training day ought to be paid, and then to say: Right! We forgot about that. We'll change it right away.

Anything you could possibly want from this company, you'd have to tell the company's customers and make them understand. You'd have to win the company's customers over to your side to get paid for the training day, but just you try getting hold of them all.

Anyway, 75 percent of the customers would probably respond to your request to get paid for the training day with: Why? I didn't get paid for my training day either.

In any case, you're sitting in a darkened training room in one of the last of seven rows of chairs. Almost all the chairs are occupied. Around you is a random collection of people of various ages dressed in dark clothing; there are plastic bags under all the chairs. Your plastic bag, which you immediately unpack, contains an orange safety vest, a blue ballpoint pen, an ice-scraper for car windows, and general information on color-printed sheets of paper. You stuff everything back in the bag, which seems to you like a cheap imitation of the freshman's pack you were given when you started college: a backpack containing a Frisbee, pens, and condoms.

You wait; everyone's waiting. Some people know each other, others start up conversations. Most of them stare into space, take their jackets off, on again, off again. You're holding a padlock for a locker. You're prepared as if for an excursion but, as I said, you're waiting, and you're no good at waiting, waiting for absolutely no reason, you want to go home again or somewhere else. So I'm telling you: You're not getting paid for the training day, but you can try and see the training day as a kind of stage play. A not very well-written stage play, because it's simply ripped off from reality, but a play nevertheless and not a training day, or maybe a training play.

So the play is called training, and it begins.

A man who has exercised his body into a state of squat firmness enters, says nothing, and exits again. A few seconds later he comes back, leans against the desk between the screen and the rows chairs, crosses his legs and arms. He's wearing well-kept, athletic-looking clothing; he exudes a scent, presumably of fabric conditioner but you might be wrong about that. A woman with pale purple streaks in her hair also enters the room, leans against the wall on the right of the audience, and smiles at the man by the desk. She's overweight and wearing a faded black T-shirt.

The man claps his hands.

Let's get started, he says. The woman goes and closes the door. Anyone who comes late has to apologize to all of us, she says, speaking half toward the audience. The man's arms dangle loosely by his sides, perhaps because they're so muscular that they don't bother him; he shows no sign of nervousness, doesn't look for a place to put his hands.

My name's Robert, he says. He speaks German with a slight American accent. I'm a qualified sports economist, he says, and I'm studying for an MBA at Leipzig University. I'm currently on an internship at Amazon. He takes a small step forward. Now I want to introduce you, though, he says to the woman still standing at the edge of the room. This is Sandy, she's an old hand, although she's still very young. How old are you, Sandy?

Thirty, says Sandy.

She's been working here, Robert continues, since the dispatch center was built. Sandy works in Dispatches, you should see her go. When she's working her arms fly incredibly fast. She looks almost like that Indian god with all the arms.

Sandy laughs.

Robert continues: As you'll have noticed, we call each other by our first names here. We're an international corporation but as you know our roots are in America. And Americans don't have a formal term of address like the German *Sie*, so we don't use it either. We're all a first-name basis from the bottom to the top, that's how it works here.

What are we doing today? He looks around but doesn't wait for an answer. Right, a training day, he says.

We've got a lot to cover.

He claps his hands again.

As he leans over the computer to start the presentation, he says that he also happens to be a semiprofessional rugby player, used to play in America. As an athlete, he takes everything as a challenge, he tells the audience. He says: Anyone who doesn't stick to the rules has to do push-ups. America is a wonderful place, but Leipzig is a wonderful place too.

He says: We at Amazon think every day is a first day. Remember that. This is a good opportunity to make a note of that and get in on the ground floor and move up. Jobs are still being filled, the company's still on the upswing but, between you and me, everyone knows nothing can grow forever. There's still plenty of potential here now, but at some point that might be different. So take your opportunity. It starts now, and you've already done a whole lot right by coming here today.

Laughter around the room. Robert switches on the projector. The Amazon website comes up on the screen. How does this look? he asks. No one answers. You feel you haven't understood the question. Hey, says Robert, remember the push-ups. So, how does this look? If no one says anything we'll be sitting here till midnight, and I don't know about you but I've got better things to do.

Someone says quietly: It doesn't look great.

Did someone say it doesn't look great? asks Robert.

A woman giggles and raises her hand.

Robert points at the projection. Nothing is supposed to be distracting, he says, and everyone is supposed to find everything right away. Even an old lady is supposed to find everything right away. And that old lady's particularly important, because if grandma can't find the cat litter she's going to close down the computer, put a crocheted cover over it, put a vase on top, and that's it. But because we're keen to get grandma's money, I'll admit it, the site is designed so that even grandma understands everything.

Robert moves to the middle of the room, the projection of the Amazon home page across his face, stretching down to the middle of his stomach. He folds his arms in front of his chest. What happens otherwise? he asks, then gives the answer himself. Grandma wants to buy kitty litter, so she goes to the store, lugs the heavy package home, and needs help carrying it upstairs, but the students on the first floor are still asleep and they can't help her. So what can grandma do? She orders from us and then the young, fit postman brings the package to her apartment door, and everyone's happy.

The audience laughs; Sandy smiles at the edge of the room. If she were a real actress she'd have to practice standing so that it didn't look awkward or lazy. You, like me, don't imagine a young, fit postman: you think of the old courier-service driver out in her rusty Ford Escort until seven or later every evening, a woman with the look of a witch about her in long, wide skirts, already past retirement age and only capable of climbing stairs to the third floor at most.

What do you think, Robert asks, what's the biggest thing Amazon's ever sold?

Sandy shrugs. A piece of the moon, she says.

Almost, says Robert, that hasn't been up for sale yet, but it will be. Then he pauses and takes a slow look around the room. He gazes slightly above the audience's heads, but it looks as though he's examining every one of you.

No, he says, what you need first is a basic course. He steps aside and points at the projection of the door on trestles. Seen this before? No one reacts, but you've seen the door before, of course; you were sitting opposite the door while you waited for your trial to start and you thought how shabby it was. You don't put your hand up; either you don't want to put your hand up or you can't manage to raise your arm. And of course you're exempted from getting involved because you're at a play, and I'll also tell you that you won't learn anything on this training day, that everything you might learn here will be explained to you again in the dispatch hall over the next two days. By that point you'll have your so-called lead worker, Norman, by your side, as muscular as Robert, and he'll like you the best out of your group of five. Your hairband with the two red bobbles on it will catch his eye and he'll call you *girl with the cherries*. You won't know right away what that means, and that it means you. But you'll know Norman means you when he responds to your question of why it has to be done the way he says and not the way it says in the instructions, which would be much easier, with the remark that you'd look much better without your thick glasses—and says nothing more than that.

So, carry on enjoying the training day and assume you won't get through your working days as unaddressed and uncommented on as this. You are, as I can say in anticipation and addition, simply one item on a list with breasts, a ponytail, and glasses.

While you were thinking about the nature of your participation in this training day, building up a definite compulsion to counter the boredom and annoyance of Robert's comments and attitude with a sudden active and above all unstoppable participation, to take the event into your own hands and instantly put an end to it, Robert has explained that the door, the door table, is a reminder that the customer is king. Is it important to the customer that I have a mahogany desk or that he gets what he wants for a good price? Does the customer want us to be sitting here on comfy sofas? Does the customer want to pay for smart offices for us? Exactly. The customer wants his order.

You'd like to contradict him, incidentally, and say: I, who am also a customer of this company, would be glad to sit more comfortably here. And I think the company could afford to provide us with more comfortable seats without having to raise prices for the customer.

You don't say that, though, because you're me and that means you're shy; you can't get your mouth open. Robert steps aside and hands over to Sandy.

Sandy says: Now you know what the customer wants. And what does Amazon want? she asks. No one answers.

Push-ups, Robert calls from the sidelines. Laughter.

Amazon wants for its employees not only to be healthy when they're working here, but also healthy when they leave the company, Sandy explains.

Right, she says, let's get moving. Everyone stands up and leaves the room, which is locked behind you. You stand there like you're in a kindergarten class, except its children have apparently grown up suddenly, all of them uncoordinated and lacking orientation. Sandy pushes through the group, taking the shortest route to the trial room you're already familiar with. You and the other participants are told to study the wall charts with safety instructions. You have to know all this, says Sandy. You try to memorize everything but your mind drifts. You look at the posters and try in vain to eavesdrop on Sandy and Robert's conversation. After ten minutes, Sandy leads the group back to the training room and waits for everyone to sit and quiet down. The screen behind her shows the rules.

Sandy knows them by heart and recites them.

Don't leave the marked paths.

Only cross the roads at the marked crossings.

Wear sturdy shoes.

Don't run, don't jog, only walk.

No loose clothing.

On hot days, knee-length pants may be worn.

For the women, Robert interjects, the rule is: please don't wear anything that gets the men so worked up they drop things.

Use the handrail.

Anyone who doesn't use the handrail has to do push-ups, says Robert. You're laughing now, he says. When I was state coach everyone had to do push-ups.

In Bad Hersfeld, says Sandy, someone managed to fall on the stairs and cut his head open. He wasn't using the handrail. We're not saying this for our own amusement.

Don't put your hands in the conveyor mechanism.

A picture of a bleeding hand comes up. This doesn't look good, says Sandy, not turning round to the screen. This is an employee's hand. He was working on the conveyor belt. When the belt stopped he put his hand inside the mechanism to adjust the slipped belt. The belt started moving again. There was a lot of screaming. This accident could have been avoided. Most accidents can be avoided.

Don't step on the pallets.

Always wear cut-resistant gloves when using cutting blades.

Lift correctly.

Anyone who doesn't lift correctly doesn't just harm themselves. Sick days harm Amazon.

Sandy repeats: We're not saying all this for our own amusement.

Robert steps up to Sandy. They look like an old TV presenter couple about to say a few warm words of farewell to their viewers. Someone's cell phone rings. A good tip, says Robert: no phones in the hall, no cameras or anything like that. Anyone who takes something like that in has to hand it over when they leave. The SIM card is removed and the phone immediately destroyed. And the punishment? asks Robert. Push-ups, answers a man in the front row.

Good luck at Amazon, says Sandy. Remember, says Robert, everyone here has done every job. Even the big boss has done what you're going to do tomorrow. Everyone here knows about everything, otherwise it wouldn't work, you see.

And so ends the play that wasn't a play, and it segues into the break, which is to be followed by your first visit to the hall. You bite into the sandwich you've brought along and pace back and forth between the training room and the entrance area. Strictly speaking, everything here is dreary and outdated and banal, and that seems to be the best disguise for a business idea to launch itself violently and expansively into the future.

Robert leads you into the changing room, where you have to choose a locker like all the others, put away your bag and jacket, and lock the door with the padlock you brought along. You're now wearing the orange safety vest, which feels far too light to be as luminous as it is. No matter how much you tug at the zipper, it keeps slipping off your shoulders.

A moment later you enter the dispatch hall, behind and in front of you other employees, also wearing safety vests. It's a kind of field trip, an excursion to unfamiliar territory, but it's a field trip that will last several weeks, and of course you'll forget it's a field trip, you'll be busy with puffing and panting and the like. But for the time being you wander the field, glad that there's finally a little exercise to be had. You wander through the security check, examined by security men. You're holding the key to your padlock in your hand but nothing beeps in the machine. You stand on a metal staircase, a chilly gallery above everyone's heads. Below you, the almost placid sight of business as usual. From above, you see an astounding order and structure, or, if you like, the deviations from this order and structure. Pallets placed out of line, bottles tipped over, cardboard fallen out of recycling bins, plastic packaging containers spilling over.

You follow the back of the man in front of you, walking down the stairs as if attached to a string, past the workers and into the warehouse area. You take automatic footsteps and look around. A mishmash of stock fills the towering shelves, the top levels only reachable by means of forklifts. This is where the stock comes to rest; the stock really seems to be sleeping and not actually for sale, as if it's reached an end there in its corners and compartments, in its random neighborhoods. You see a dust-coated stock museum; you like it. The things on the shelves, silence reigning around them because no one is here to collect them and send them to the customer, radiate sobriety and are something like the dabs on a painting, something with nothing threatening about it, nothing mechanical. The products look like retired former workers for this global corporation. You don't quite understand how a fortune could be made out of these things on either side of you and out of books and data carriers and a program and a website, a fortune that's still growing. Nor do you understand why that fortune is not allowed to have a reverse effect on the hall, to add a little comfort or shine. It's not as if you don't realize the fact that the fortune is deliberately prevented from flowing back toward the employees; you simply don't understand it, and of course it can't be understood.

You're given a pair of work shoes. There are two different kinds, one with blue markings and the other with orange; all of them have large air holes in them. You try on the shoes like a chance discovery, like shoes you've found in some kind of donation pile. You might think what I thought at the time—of New York, of Coney Island, where I spotted shoes under a pier on the beach, an incredible amount of shoes. I couldn't imagine where the pile of shoes might have come from or why it was there in the first place. I stood in front of it for a very long time, not touching any of the shoes even though there were some very nice, undamaged-looking shoes in the pile. It was only in my hotel room that night that I realized the pile had consisted solely of shoes for left feet.

You slip into the work shoes; they're spacious and stiff but you'll soon wear them in and stop laughing at them like they're a disguise. Sandy urges you all to get a move on and everyone folds up their shoe boxes, throws them in the paper recycling container, and marches after Sandy. An orange employee caterpillar with billowing edges crawls out of the hall in a somehow cheerful mood, lines up at the security check, and casts off its color ready to leave.

So you're now a seasonal associate with a locker of your own at Amazon, and you'll soon be home. Outside the drugstore in the city center, a reporter approaches you with a microphone. You stop because you can't dodge him and the microphone is almost touching your nose. Good afternoon, says the reporter. You stare straight ahead and listen to his voice, a trained reporter's voice that seems to require no body, a voice too perfect to come out of a person and not immediately and solely out of a radio, a voice that says to you: Guinness World Record Day is coming up soon. Aha, you say. Have you heard of it? asks the voice. No, you say and you want to go on walking but from ahead of you come tourists with suitcases and from behind you a group of school kids push past. What record would you like to hold? asks the reporter. None, you say, I don't want to hold a record. You don't have the faintest idea why anyone should hold a record. It's a question for children, and you tell that to the reporter, you tell him to catch up with the school kids, but, of course, on closer consideration you realize: you wish you were the richest woman in town. Or at least the richest woman in your neighborhood.

As it happens, your parents are lottery players, so you're familiar with the hope for money, the expectation of money.

It'll soon arrive and it will come from somewhere, that's what you believe and at the same time you're constantly contradicting that belief, trying to persuade yourself against it. But something inside you believes unshakably that a huge pile of money will one day come to you, far exceeding any demand for unconditional basic income and with no connection to any work you might have to perform. Something inside you dreams ready-made dreams; you'll have to take a look at that soon and read about it in Bloch, for example. We can do that later.

Three

You're still at home at noon; you're working the late shift. No one's in the apartment. You already miss your desk, even though you're standing right next to it. You go to the bedroom and hang up socks on the drying rack. You're slow, as though in a land consisting only of stretching time that fills itself. You seem like you're ready to move backward in time—but where do you want to go? You can't think of anywhere, off the bat. You're spinning around in the past, which is neither yours nor mine, traveling in a time that really is time, a treasure chest for surplus hours of calm and happiness; really, you're caught in a kind of poetry. You're managing something you rarely do because you're usually so diverted and scatterbrained. Now that you have to leave any minute, you feel like you have to step out of a mild summer's day into a snowstorm.

Are you exaggerating?
    On the one hand, yes.
    On the other hand, no.
    You're not exaggerating one bit. You're right.

I'm thinking of a job I once had, but hardly any of those jobs is worth remembering, and before I do any more remembering I'd rather think of Monika Maron's book

Stille Zeile Sechs and the protagonist Rosa's question of whether she should get paid for thinking or not, and her answer that she doesn't want to think in return for payment, which doesn't work, though—or, rather, she gets a job where she doesn't have to think and it's not demanded of her, but she still thinks nonetheless, albeit differently than before.

In any case, you're on the tram now, nearly there. The tram passes the Erotic Center. Its façade is brightly lit, with a buxom, confident, and cozy-looking naked woman painted larger than life on one side. She, you instantly realize, is your friend. Your large confidante is the silent type but you could talk to her, you'd almost swear.

You get to the warehouse early, so you turn around and go for a little walk. You pretend it's possible to take a walk in this area. You end up in a DIY superstore, sit down in the in-house bakery café, and think briefly of all the things that happened in the past, or of whatever. Then you get up, knock back your coffee, and burn your tongue and your throat.

You, until I think otherwise, are courageous and strong, and I, until I think otherwise, am the opposite of you. I didn't walk briskly to the gate, I tarried for a while, but you, you go right ahead; nothing can happen to you. Nothing ever befalls you. If that's not the case, if that's too boldly formulated, I'll just put it like this: Nothing will happen to you here, not today, that's for sure; I can't see any further ahead than that.

You look a little different now. You're wearing your clunky work shoes and you look down on the shoes from above, twist one foot, examine the sole. You thread the locker key onto a ribbon and hang it around your neck. You carry the luminous vest in one hand, not putting it on right away. That's your sign of not belonging, a small luxury that interests no one, an act for which you'll soon have no time.

You cross the line of employees waiting for their shifts to begin so that you can wait in the cafeteria to be picked up for your first day at work. You sit down with the others who are new like you are. Outside in the corridor, the security woman calls out that people are only allowed to queue directly by the turnstile after two fifteen. Until then, everyone has to wait in the corridor between the cafeteria and the changing rooms. She yells: How often do I have to tell you that!

Incidentally, people here will talk to you like I sometimes talk to my children, something like this:
    Get up!
    Be quiet!
    Get dressed!
    Eat!

Lie down!
Close your eyes!
Go to sleep!
Stop that!

So there you sit, and you have workmates. Stefanie, a retail saleswoman from Grimma who wants to start training with the German railroad corporation, says: I've experienced more boring things than yesterday's training day.

Grit says: I'm not going to do push-ups. I'm a trainer myself but I don't use methods like that. I believe in tough words, not stupid punishments. She has a clear, strict voice. She wears her hair in a tight ponytail and her bangs are cut into a curve, its highest point above her left eyebrow and tailing down toward her right ear.

Stefanie looks at her watch and says: They might as well get started. I'm not surprised my order arrived late the other week, they don't seem to take punctuality all that seriously.

Grit says: No one has to wait this long at my place. The place she means is the restaurant in the basement of the town hall in Torgau, which is apparently closed right now for conversion, from serving old-fashioned German cuisine to steaks.

Hans-Peter, about sixty years old with a remarkable similarity to an East German actor whose name you can't recall, gives an angry laugh and says: And then they'll take you back, will they?

Yes, says Grit, my boss calls me up every few days and says it's nearly time to open up again, tells me not to get rusty.

You won't have time to get rusty, says Hans-Peter, they won't keep us here for long.

You ask him how long he wants to stay. At least until spring, says Hans-Peter, then there'll be work in Halle again. He's wearing a faded old pair of overalls; nothing in the cafeteria is as old as those overalls.

Florian comes dashing into the cafeteria, too late, and he'll always be late. Are you here for the induction day? he asks. Hans-Peter nods. Florian sits down and stretches his legs out under the table, only to pull them back in immediately and stand up and dash to the changing rooms to get changed. Hey, he calls on his way out, I'll be right back.

Hans-Peter says: They won't keep him on, that's for sure.

Norman arrives slightly late, says hello, and gives a brief wave to encourage you and your workmates to get up. You walk behind him, at first as a loose crowd, forming a well-arranged line at the turnstile. He says hello to people here and there as he walks; he has a comfortable pace, you'll never see him rushing anywhere. The first level of managers sit at the lead desk. Norman makes you and your workmates wait there, so you stand around and tug at your safety vest, and you don't put on a nice smile because you're not like that; it'd be more like me to smile almost apologetically into the unknown.

Like your new workmates, you're handed a box, containing a cutter, cut-resistant gloves, a fish knife, a marker, rubber bands, Post-its, a pencil, and a cleaning cloth. Everyone is supposed to use the marker to write their name on the box and then put the box on a shelf. Your box lines up there alongside others. You look at your box with your scribbled name on it and think of capsule hotels and miniature residential cabins. The box is a tiny place.

You trot after Norman as he leads you around the hall. Two forklift drivers accompany your group, disappearing between the shelves, popping up again at the end of an aisle, blocking the way, joking around with Norman, who sends them away: Haven't you got anything better to do?

Not much up today, one of them says.

I've got plenty to do though, Norman says.

You watch your working time melt away, but you also register with interest that working time is allowed to simply melt away at Amazon, that there isn't a light that goes on some place in the company to signal wasted working time to a supervisor and order immediate countermeasures. So this is what you make a mental note of: between the shelves, in the empty halls, beyond the lead desks, outside of the glass container they want to demolish soon, where the more important bosses and planners sit at their desks, working time is allowed to melt away; there are places where you can be slow.

Not that speed is picking up now, already. Everything's still calm. You're sitting in a small training room inside a metal container, a second floor balanced on top of another metal container. Austere furnishings, everyone sitting around one table, leftover writing still legible on the board.

Norman splays out his fingers so hard his joints make cracking noises, and then puts laminated cards down on the table like a dealer. He tells the group to pick a card in clockwise order, explain the pictogram on their card, and then replace it.

Grit is holding a card showing an arrow. She shrugs.

But that's a perfect one for women, Norman says, you always see that on furniture boxes. No response from Grit.

Even I know that one, Hans-Peter says.

The arrow shows which way is up, says Norman, annoyed. You must know that. You women always love going to IKEA.

You bite your tongue to stop yourself from contradicting him. Actually, no, it's not like that, of course. You're courageous and brave, so you open your mouth and say: Could you formulate that differently, please, sir? I don't like it when sentences start with *you women*, because that kind of sentence usually conceals grossly generalizing, limiting assumptions, or doesn't even conceal them, shows them openly and clearly. So I suggest you use the following sentence: This pictogram is found on packaging material, for example on boxes containing items of furniture like you can buy at IKEA, among other places.

Yes, Norman would say, Little Miss Professor, we can make all this a little bit more polite.

Or: We're all on a first-name basis here, no need for the sir, just call me Norman.

Or, most likely: No need to get offended.

In your place, I didn't say anything, just thought that the history of the world is often one thing above all: a collection of moments judged as inappropriate; inappropriate for addressing something, explaining something, fighting for something, arguing something. There's always someone biting their tongue.

You need a breath of fresh air; you say you need the bathroom. You walk around, go for a stroll, allow yourself the pleasure. Further forward, below the turnstile, it's loud in the hall, but above it the noise is calm, a person might be able to think there—though maybe that's not the case.

You go back and Norman asks if you fainted. Florian is missing. He's on drugs, says Grit, he's gone to shoot up.

He's always fidgeting, says Stefanie.

That's what I said, says Hans-Peter, he'll be out of here before we can blink an eye. You're surprised; you hadn't noticed any of that. Norman puts the cards away, reads out pedantic safety instructions and makes you sign that you've heard all the instructions. You sit and wait.

And apart from that, Norman says, you'll manage it. It's not as strict as it looks here, maybe you'll be taken on permanently. Right, he says, lunch break.

All the employees, it appears, rush to the exit at once. You end up in a jumble of people, where it's impossible not to be touched. Everyone makes a play of pushing as close as possible up to the others, as though they might walk through their coworkers to pass through the turnstile faster. The queue picks up speed again just before the detectors and untangles, the hall spits out employees for their break the way a ball machine spews out balls. So you stare upward, waiting for the green light signaling that the turnstile can be entered. The old-timers start walking when the light's still red. Although there's no rule about leaving for a break as quickly as possible, everybody does it.

You eat, and soon you'll be gobbling your food down. A man a few tables down is reading. You'd like to know what he's reading but you can't make it out. You always what to know what random people are reading. You always want to possess books. You may even want to possess all books.

You go back into the hall, making sure to walk past the security woman with your head held high, which she doesn't even notice because she stares right through you, as she does through everyone wearing their safety shoes and safety vests as the regulations require. A board just before the staircase down to the hall displays the status of the expected bonus payments: estimated 3 percent bonus.

Near to your box of work tools, you wait for Norman and your coworkers and you look around. But I'm going to give you the afternoon off even before your colleagues and coworkers arrive, because why shouldn't I give you an afternoon off? I'm happy to give you an afternoon off, and I hereby give time off to everyone who'd like some time off.

At the very moment when I give you the afternoon off, though, the shift is discontinued due to lack of work, so you don't make it out of the hall alone after all. Sorry about that. Your workmates push and shove you up the stairs. You'll soon be walking as fast and pushing and shoving as much as them, you'll develop methods to block the way of colleagues who push past too aggressively or to elbow them as you pass.

You take off your work shoes and your feet grow light again. You're glad to be leaving early. You think: I wouldn't mind if it stayed this way. And of course you're right about that.

At the tram stop, a cold easterly wind pinches your cheeks. You turn your back to it.

While you trundle back to town on the tram and later spend a little while watching a log fire flickering on a flat screen through a window onto a hotel foyer, I call a friend on the phone.

It's really getting on my nerves, my friend says, I don't know what to do about it. Is it me or the work or my coworkers? Really, my friend says on the phone, the learning curve's going right down, it's just dull and far too difficult at the same time. And no one understands that I'm not interested in working more to make more money. I really don't see the offer to work more in the long-term as a compliment, more as an imposition.

Another friend says she actually doesn't want to work any more, she just doesn't want to, not one little bit, and if she didn't need the money she wouldn't work, not in her job, or she'd completely remodel her job and change her colleagues, she'd work with people who like what they do. Then she'd enjoy working again.

You haven't got that far yet, you're still capable of being objective and telling differences, but in a few weeks' time you'll say: But that's not what it's about. It's not about fun and enjoyment, not at all. I don't get that out of it either.

You won't talk the way you normally talk, by then. You'll end up talking to yourself in employee language.

Four

I read an essay by Claudia Friedrich Seidel, which begins with an admission: "Yes," she writes, "I too buy my books from Amazon.com."

Yes, I say, I too buy my books from Amazon. I buy the books there that I can't get elsewhere. What I don't buy from Amazon is books or other things I *can* get elsewhere, not even if they're cheaper there or delivered more quickly.

A few days before, I held a far too vehement lecture at my mother's kitchen table, preaching that one doesn't necessarily have to buy things one wants from the cheapest source. I said there was no order and no law that you have to choose the cheapest offer. My mother looked at me as though checking whether I meant it seriously, first of all, and secondly whether I might have turned into a rich woman overnight, someone who could afford to say such things.

I think of a writer I know, a woman who tries on everything in the stores in town before buying anything, and then orders the clothes later at home from online retailers having nothing to do with the stores in town. She says: I'm not going to give the stores anything. She says it seriously and a little stubbornly. She might as well say: I'm not going to let them rip me off over the counter. And so she prefers to buy from places where there are no counters, and the counter where the customer is ripped off or lured in or simply contacted is the customer's own desk or kitchen counter or notebook table; that is, if the customer's not simply balancing their computer on their lap or holding their tablet in their hand.

In any case, my boyfriend has mail from Amazon. Two children carry the parcel around the apartment, not understanding, just as I don't, why the parcel doesn't get unpacked right away. My boyfriend rescues his parcel and eventually tells us what's in there: pants. Our older son complains and wants something too, and the younger one keeps on lugging the parcel around; it's almost as big as he is. Two pairs of pants, says my boyfriend, and each pair was thirty euros cheaper than in the store.

Each pair? I ask.

Each pair, he says.

Damn, I say.

Days later, I spy the parcel in the hallway again, its corners slightly dented, ready for returning. The pants were the wrong color, my boyfriend says. They weren't dark blue, they were blue-black. I shrug, kind of glad he didn't manage to save sixty euros that easily, but perhaps that's not true either. Perhaps I don't care either, and anyway we're not talking about these two pairs of pants bought by my boyfriend, we're talking, for example, about the bluffs and cheats that Hannes Hintermeier described in a rather old article in the *Frankfurter Allgemeine Zeitung*, using the example of a nonfiction author who preferred to remain anonymous. This author, I read, "hated Amazon, with the full force of his passion. He preached that we ought to stand up to the monopolist with all our might. Admittedly, whenever he wanted a book, he simply told his wife and she ordered it for him—from Amazon."

You won't be packaging dispatches that reach that nonfiction writer or me or anyone else. You'll be receiving goods inward and entering them in the warehousing system, so that the products can then be ordered. And it will take a while before you get deployed in the book section, which incidentally is mainly reserved for women, like reading novels once was. When you come to enter the myriads of books into the system you might be glad of it, or you might not. We'll see when the time comes.

I was always glad, at any rate, to stand beside the gigantic book boxes and enter the books in the system, I looked at the books and knew what kind of thing the Germans buy, so, for example, I knew the Germans like to buy the humorous health writer Eckart von Hirschhausen, because I had a hundred copies of Eckart von Hirschhausen's face on my desk and put them in a yellow crate. And I found out there really are an incredible number of vampire novels, something I could have guessed beforehand but wouldn't have thought possible.

I was glad of the books every day at Amazon, but one day I found myself with a book in my hands written by a man I know, formerly a good friend of mine. I got a shock; it was an absolutely unexpected encounter between him and me. There in the dispatch hall, where I placed approximately forty of his books in the crate for preordered products—meaning I knew what people would read and what they considered a good Christmas gift—it was as if I were the chambermaid and he were the guest. It was as if we were showing our true faces. At first I thought nothing, and after that I thought simpleminded things. I measured my life against his with the yardstick of, which I didn't have, unlike him. The man is part of the world in which a person can feed a wife and child by working a job he enjoys. With his book in my hands, I didn't want to think much and I didn't think much. I thought: I bet he has time right now to think about his next work; it would have to be called a *work*, and he'd have to be called a *successful writer*.

You, though, are now waiting at the meeting place by the shelf full of boxes in the dispatch hall, clutching your box of work tools and really on the serious side of life. You're waiting around in the consequences drawn from your financial situation and the opportunities on the so-called labor market. Cold air streams past you. You pull the fleece jacket you're wearing under the safety vest up to your chin, put the hood over your head. One of the gates to the dock doesn't close reliably. That's how it will stay and by the time you're pretty much broken down you'll be told the company won't bring in a heater for your sake. You'll say you don't want a heater. But then, by the time you're really broken down, you won't be able to explain calmly what exactly you asked for (for the gate to be repaired at long last). You'll notice a trembling that hasn't come about deep inside you just at that moment, but instead has been trembling away for a while and is spreading to your limbs. You're still looking ahead to a time of misunderstandings.

You examine the growing crowd of colleagues waiting for the shift to start, and you spot your workmates Grit and Stefanie. The two of them are chatting about the previous day. You join them, stand next to them, and there's something very old inside you, something that comes from me, which I hereby hand over to you so that you can deal with it, give it the full treatment and get it over and done with once and for all. You wish the two women would include you in their little circle. You want that very much for a few seconds. But Grit and Stefanie barely look at you and don't move a muscle to make space for you. They tighten up, and we'll come back later to what you wanted here for a moment, to this wanting to belong, we'll come back to the way everyone here wants at their core to belong, which is mainly because no one has any time left to belong elsewhere.

For the time being, there's nothing about you that interests Grit and Stefanie. The two of them have become a team overnight and Hans-Peter also has a new friend, whom he's telling nearby about how he nearly had a severe accident on the autobahn just now. His new friend says yes and aha and oh boy and sounds involved and absent at the same time. You don't say anything.

The managers are gradually gathering in the middle of the crowd. They're marked by their clipboards and colored lanyards and by the fact that they have enough space to position their legs in a commanding manner. The employees' conversations gradually fall silent and everyone turns to the bosses. You take a few steps back to get to the outer edge of this gathering—which reminds you of a flag ceremony except it's not held along the angular lines painted on the floor of a gymnasium, but as a loosely woven circle three to five people deep. You step back as far as possible from the area where the bosses are standing.

A bell rings to start the shift and the shift manager Mirko takes half a step forward out of the line of managers. He stands with his legs wide and taps the side of his clipboard against his left palm.

Welcome to the late shift, he says. As you can see, the docks are empty, but it won't stay that way for long, we're approaching our peak week. We haven't got all that many inbound goods today, it should be a quiet shift. We have to make sure we leave something for the early shift to do, but it should be fine. We're expecting a few deliveries. He pauses briefly and then continues. Good news: Amazon Italy opened today. There were seven orders in the first five minutes—a good start, I'd say.

He looks around. Any safety tips? he asks.

You adjust your first impression. This isn't a variation on a flag ceremony, it's more of an American motivational huddle, like before a basketball game, except that the staff aren't athletic and glamorous, just standing around in a very wooden, un-American way.

Right, says the shift manager, then I've got a tip. Please park your cars parallel to each other. We have to make optimum use of the parking lot now. We've got a lot of new staff. And keep an eye on the footpaths. Pedestrians have right of way.

He nods and taps the clipboard against his hand again. Have a good shift.

Most people go to their workstations. Hans-Peter, Grit, Stefanie, and you wait for Norman. That parking lot's chaos, says Hans-Peter, you can't get here early enough to make it in time, and you should see how some people park, all over the place and five attempts at hitting the spot. He comes up close to you; you retreat slightly. He reaches into the chest pocket of his overalls and takes out a packet of tablets. He looks at you in such a way that you know he expects something of you, something to do with the tablets.

Did you steal them? you ask.

Hans-Peter reduces the distance between you and taps his forefinger against his lips. Tooth abscess, he says.

Oh, you say. Hans-Peter explains that his tooth actually needs operating on but he's pushed the operation back now.

But aren't you in pain? you ask.

Sure I am, Hans-Peter replies, or I wouldn't need this stuff—he pats his pocket.

You'd be better off at home then, you say.

Well I can't stay home, I can't, I've got to be here now, Hans-Peter says.

But if you're sick? you say.

You could talk that way forever and you will talk that way a few more times, and in a few days—once you've got sick and then recovered again and you're told to work right next to the roller door that doesn't shut properly so that a coworker of yours doesn't have to work there—you'll go to that workmate and say you've just been sick so you really want to work in a warm spot and not in a draft. He'll shrug and you'll realize he's sick right there and then, his eyes are watering. You'll put your hand on his forehead and feel how hot he is. You should go home, you'll say. He'll shrug again and say he wants to be taken on permanently, though. You'll repeat that he ought to go home but he won't be put off, and you'll end up working in the draft—shivering, sweating, shivering.

Hans-Peter says he shouldn't actually be driving on his tablets. You say he's risking too much for the job. Easy for you to say, he says. So you say exactly what Hans-Peter needs to hear so he can say exactly what he wants to say.

Norman comes over at his comfortable pace and gestures as though your group had turned up late. He herds you all further into the hall, to an area where no one else is working. All the workstations are free. He knocks on the tabletop. Right, he says. A forklift passes; the driver stops close to your group, loads up empty pallets and drives on. The group and Norman wave as though they were the first and last people in this gigantic hall. The workstation is tall and dusty on the edge of the tabletop, with dust on the shelves beneath it. A second workstation is adjoined to it. In this part of the hall, the workstations are grouped in pairs, fenced in by a network of lines as yet incomprehensible to you, intended to mark where pallets have to go, alongside inbound goods to be logged, already logged and ready to be picked up by the forklift drivers. Next to the workstation are large cardboard boxes, dented and misshapen containers for separate disposal of ripped up boxes and plastic packaging.

Norman divides the group into two smaller groups. Grit and Stefanie are allotted a lead worker who picks them up and takes them to other desks. You'd rather go with them but you have to work in Norman's group with Hans-Peter and Florian, who hasn't turned up yet, though nobody's waiting for him. The task you have to learn is this: remove the product from its box, check the product's packaging or the product itself for damage, scan the product's barcode, put the logged product on another pallet or in a *tote*, and always pay attention to the computer, which tells you want to do and what everything's name is.

Here are the names of some things you'll do and how you'll have to refer to them:

Tote
ASIN
Scan tote
Scan ASIN
Scan ASINs until enough in tote
Tote full
Next tote

Tote—what does that sound like? says Hans-Peter. Let me tell you something you might not know: In German, *tote* sounds like the word for dead or death. It's like working in a crematorium, says Hans-Peter. You don't want to use these new terms quite yet, but Norman makes it clear: You can call the tote a crate, but it won't help you much because the tote's called a tote and it's called a tote everywhere. It's better to remember it right away.

Florian comes dashing in. Norman doesn't say anything, just stands silently in front of him, a punishing father who can't find the right words but conveys his low opinion of Florian entirely with his silence.

You go on trying out the new words.

Tote.
ASIN.
Mark defective.
Cubi.
Problem solver.
MHD goods.
Prep.

Nothing feels real, not even the consignment of goods a forklift operator drops off beside you. Two pallets piled with shrink-wrapped brown cardboard boxes. Right now, you're in the middle of real employee life and at the same time you're in the continuation of the game that began at the test session. Norman tells Florian and Hans-Peter to release the shrink-wrap with their fish knives. They've hardly begun before he intervenes; they're working too slowly and carefully for his taste. He releases the plastic from the boxes with fast, rough movements, rips it off, balls it up, and tosses it overarm straight into the plastics container. He opens a box and pulls out a package printed with a shiny wheel rim, more throws than places it on the workstation, and elucidates the situation. Right, he says, we've got a box full of the same product. Then we leave the product in there, we don't take them all out, only one of them to scan the barcode, if you can't find it on the outside of the box. Takes too long otherwise. He moves the box around until he finds the barcode and then scans it. Watch me, he says, I'm not doing this for my own sake, I can do all this already. He enters the number of wheel rim boxes contained in the brown cardboard box. Then it looks as though the desk were throwing the brown box at Norman so that he can put the wheel rim back into its container with verve, taking no care to protect the edges. There's nothing obviously special about his motions; all you notice is the absolute unspecialness of them. Norman's movements follow a strict sense of timing; he seems to use the exact same amount of time for each activity, everything is subordinated to his sense of time, and each product to be processed is merely something that impairs the adherence to time requirements more or less than others.

You say: But how are we supposed to check the product for damage if we don't take it out of the box, if we only look at one product out of many and just count the rest?

Norman rolls his eyes. Little Miss Professor, he says, you go ahead and take them all out if you like.

In the midst of the other newbies, you're in an unknown land with an unknown language and the person who's supposed to show you everything doesn't understand what a stranger doesn't know or can't know and what has to be explained to you. Norman says: You don't have to understand it, by the way, you just have to know it.

Norman puts you to work next to Hans-Peter. Florian works at the desk opposite you. You hand the products to Hans-Peter so he can scan the barcode from the packaging. You count the items and stow them on the pallet for the warehouse. You work slowly because Hans-Peter is having trouble with the computer. He can't place the cursor where he wants it, using the mouse. His cursor chases nervously around its target. You help him on the computer, explain what you think you've understood. I might be wrong, you say. You minimize the window, which Hans-Peter maximized to be too large to handle.

He puts his hand on yours and you pull your hand away. He leans over the keyboard, looks at you from below, stands bent down like at an aquarium so he can look at you closely, puts on a grin and says: Give us a smile.

I've already mentioned that even if you're usually a man, you're a woman in this situation, and that's the way it is.

Not being me, you don't take a step back. You tell him to stop it right away.

Or else? Hans-Peter asks.

Or else nothing, you say. Just stop it. There's nothing more to say. Seeing as you're you and you can take a sharp tone when you want to, Hans-Peter stops staring at your face like a playful scientist while you're trying to help him with the computer. He's now distracted, anyway, by the warning sounds issuing from Florian's computer at the next desk. Norman, who was just with Grit and Stefanie and their lead worker, rushes over, positions himself next to Florian and watches him. Florian runs a nervous hand through his hair and taps away at the keyboard like a wild thing. I'm not saying anything, Norman says.

Please say something, Florian asks him.

No, I'm not saying anything, Norman repeats.

Another great start, Florian says, more to himself than to Norman. He's got a reputation in his own mind—he'll confirm that reputation in the briefest of periods, and then he'll stop showing up for work.

Norman presses Escape and the computer shuts up. He laughs. Florian says to Norman: I don't sweat as much as you.

I'm not sweating at all, says Norman.

You feel like you're just about part of a group. A group that's been thrown out of the saddle by a galloping donkey. Or by the cynical solemnity of a misunderstood working life.

You're playing with the products—or what is it you're doing? You're learning something about the products and how to deal with them.

You have to use strips of tape to cover up the so-called touch cutouts in the packaging of protective car-seat covers. You have to bag up unpackaged suitcases and make sure the bags have air holes. You come across a glass bathtub duck with a barcode not recognized by the computer. A new product, says Norman. You take a closer look as you're carrying it across the hall, barely noticing the floor markings. You're carrying a glass bathtub duck; neither you nor I can say anything else about that.

You're supposed to log a crate full of advent calendars into the system, but they're advent calendars filled with tea bags. Every tea bag has a drawing of a politician's face on it, intended to peep out over the edge of a cup once the calendar reaches the customer. You carry the crate of calendars over to the MHD department, where all food-stuffs are processed.

You come across a hairdryer with the name Alpine Hairdryer Grossglockner. You can't help laughing. You repeat the product name but Hans-Peter doesn't think there's anything funny about it, merely commenting that you are capable of laughing after all.

You rip up cardboard boxes; that's the hardest part. Norman comes over, takes a cardboard box, rips it into pieces, and throws it in with the used cardboard. You yawn inside as he does so.

Other than that, you're refreshing your old knowledge of the working world in here. You won't come across anything you don't already know from what your parents have told you.

You work, put the cut-resistant gloves on and take them off, you explain over and over to Hans-Peter how the computer works, you stare at the screen, sometimes you drop a product, and then you get a shock and hope it's not broken. You don't yet know the most important thing: Workers have to treat the products like a slave-driver treats slaves. After all, you're working here in a multilayered and complex system of dominances, and you always have to decide who you want to be. The question for every day is: Do you want the products to lead you around by the nose?

It's a matter of the prestige a person can obtain. It's a matter of the unpopular status of the lowest-ranking slave, which no one wants. So it's a matter of treating the products roughly, so that they don't rise up above the workers. You'll learn that soon enough, but you'll never be much good at it.

Later, you wait twenty minutes for the tram. When it finally arrives you stand pressed close to your colleagues, standing like a battered dog in the warmth, framed by fogged-up windowpanes. You get caught in a cycle of reading the print on the bag belonging to a woman you don't know, standing ahead of you: Summer Spirit. You read it over and over, read it until the woman gets off at the station. You get off the tram as well and see the woman running to the station entrance; running seems absurd at this time of day. You don't take the direct route home; you walk slowly toward the center of town.

The bike stands next to Lehmann's bookstore are wrapped in different shades of knitted wool, some of it neon bright. It's called guerilla knitting; you read about it a while ago. Of course, there's nothing rebellious or militant about this knitting, about wrapping wool around bike stands. You think it's just kind of annoying and dumb. A woolen protest that isn't a protest, intended to show that the world should be a more colorful place; you don't have much time at the moment, and for you it's a symbol of a great smart-ass waste of time. You don't understand how anyone can spend so much time knitting around bike stands, how anyone could knit a thousand stitches and then sew them around bike stands. And why make it so decorative? you ask yourself. It's just before midnight, your feet are aching, and you're in a bad mood.

Five

You go for a walk in the park. You walk around aimlessly, stocking up on fresh air. You know it's Sunday and that Monday follows Sunday and that Monday brings the start of a week of early shifts. The local ducks have swum a hole in their frozen pond. Your feet are very cold. Soon, once snow falls and that snow puts the morning city out of action, it will feel as though those feet, aching with cold, are your biggest problem.

Right now, though, things are kind of alright. You put on a show of pragmatism—you'll just have to buy better shoes once you've got some money together again. You're not yet thinking all day long that you'd rather not go to work. Nor are you inventing excuses for why you can't, coming up with reasons why you can't go to work that particular day, why you absolutely cannot go. But I can still see the little evasion: you don't want to go home, you don't want to move into the evening that then leads into the night and from there to the morning, which is a Monday morning.

You walk some more. Ahead of you, you see people you know, so you turn around—you don't want to run into anyone you know—and you almost slip on the wooden bridge over the pond. You're in a bad mood, that's how Sunday evenings are in the working world, in this working world I'm talking about.

You walk to the river, where a musician with the croaky voice is playing his keyboard. A loner, an untiring soul, always there or at some other spot, and always singing the wrong lyrics. You think: Can't he practice? But he won't practice. Someone usually ends up laughing at him, but it never gets through to him. He seems to think he's always on the brink of justified discovery. Not a doubt ever crosses his mind. You may well know that feeling, but you as me aren't familiar with it.

In the end, you do run into some people you haven't seen for years. He's an internist, she's a hematologist, and they've moved back from Switzerland with their new baby. The two of them invite you back to their place for a glass of mulled wine, and you say yes. You work out you now live close to each other. The couple live in a sweeping late-nineteenth-century building on one side of the square, and you at the other end, in the last concrete block built in your East German city under the socialist system, constructed in an experimental style, which in this case means that the building you live in attempts to emulate the old buildings around it with their slanted roofs and decorated external walls. Before you enter their house, the couple say: How practical, next time we can come to you.

Yes of course, you say, and you climb the polished stairs to the couple's large, in fact gigantic apartment. You know gigantic apartments, and you know good furniture too—you haven't known them all your life, but you've got to know good furniture and you can distinguish furniture that wants to look like good furniture from furniture that really is good. The couple show you around, talking. You walk around the apartment and gradually lose track of what's going on. You sense the two of them always do this, they have a reflexive need to show off and they don't know there's no need to impress you, don't realize you're no competition. But after the second glass of mulled wine, which you drink far too quickly, you feel an approximate challenge to a duel and you turn down the medium-priced chocolates placed on the table. You say: I only eat Pierre Marcolini Belgian chocolates, they're the best. They cost 30 euros a box, but they're worth it. The couple get you to repeat the name of the chocolates. You don't normally lie, but you could go on lying now. You could fill an entire evening with lies, just like that, and only stop once the couple had filled a sheet of A4 paper with notes and brand names. You choose to stop talking instead. Above the cradle, in which the couple's son is grabbing his feet and breathing in sighs, is a photo of the same child wrapped in a blanket. Next to the child is an old copy of Adorno's *Minima Moralia*; the baby's tiny forefinger, stretched out, seems to want to open the book. You think of Emil Cioran, who was surprised that anyone could delight in the sight of a newborn child, that anyone could be glad of the birth of a child at all, being of the view that one ought to cry at the birth of a child, instead. You ask the couple whether they've read Cioran.

It's time for you to leave, in other words. You stand up and bump your head on the lamp hanging above the table and the lamp swings back at you again; you hold your forehead. Do you know these people well? You're standing across from them and you don't know the answer to that question. Perhaps you confused them with another couple. This will be your last meeting, at any rate; you know that and the couple know it too. The couple say: You must come by again some time.

You say: We really do live very close.

The man makes a joke and you laugh, even though you've heard the joke before, in a better version. Then you walk down the creaking stairs, cross the square with its sumptuous old buildings, and switch over to a different world.

You're alone in the apartment now. To begin with, I pretended you had my boyfriend and my children, but that's not how it is. I'm not going to share them. I can't do that. You're me, but you don't have my entire life. So in principle you're alone in the apartment, but I'm there too.

You sit down at the desk for a while. You could write an invoice, it occurs to you, there's still one unwritten, but you don't do it. You're working tomorrow morning, so you fold up your little weekend, go into the bathroom, and then you go to bed with a bowl of pasta. Forking it into your mouth, you stare at the TV, not registering much. You just stare. On Sundays you're like a child who doesn't like school, hoping for a sickness that will keep you home tomorrow. In any case, though, you have a short week ahead of you; you just don't know it yet. You'll get sick after only two days and sign off with your manager, and you'll be surprised at how politely he wishes you a speedy recovery.

You take the bowl back to the kitchen, reciting the words of my early-shift father: Oh, nine already, it's off to bed for me then. Then you lie down and aren't the slightest bit tired. You toss and turn and pull the covers over your head for a while. The night before your next working day lies ahead of you like a test of your courage. In two to four years' time, you'll be different, you'll have had enough of all fear, no company or anyone else will squeeze you under the covers, wide awake at a child's bedtime. But for now you lie there like I lay there, and you try to put yourself into a sensible employee's sleep.

While you twist and turn, a bed comes together in your mind, a metabed, at first more comfortable than the real bed, and you lie down in this mental bed and are far away from Sunday and Monday, far from the sequence of days; there are no days. So a bed comes about in your mind, a bed you'll seek out during the day not long from now, while clearly and visibly standing and working in the dispatch hall. It happens automatically, you don't even notice it. In the end, when it's time to stop being a seasonal associate before the end of your contract, you'll have filled this bed up with trash—there'll be crumpled paper, vodka bottles, condoms, cigarette butts, and a small, absolutely unfamiliar toy dog gathered around its edges. Your mental bed will look like Tracey Emin's bed, in which the artist spent a long period of depression after the end of a relationship, but your mental bed won't be sold at Christie's for £2.5 million like Tracey Emin's bed, you'll have to clean it up yourself later. You'll be embarrassed; the bed will seem to you like a deathbed. The bed in your mind will give you the creeps and then you'll tidy it up, you'll stuff all the trash in plastic bags, take the bags away, and imagine yourself throwing the bags out.

So to return to the question from the beginning, about whether it's a matter of life and death, I'm now saying clearly: Yes, it is.

You, in your beds, think you need at least fourteen hours' sleep. That impression is wrong, of course, but you'd still hold an impassioned plea not to cope without those extra hours, on this night in particular. I, on the other hand, am wide awake at the kitchen table, inhabiting the night you sleep through, and I'm remembering a feast at an incredibly long table, with a seating plan that placed men and women next to each other, alternating. The food tasted bland but looked elaborate: sugar coatings, nitrogen steam spouting from jugs, a pool of chocolate sauce in the shape of the hosts' silhouettes. Across the aspiring mayor to my right, a woman told me about her daughter, who was my age. The daughter herself was sitting diagonally opposite her and put her hand over her wine glass as soon as a wine bottle approached her vicinity. She was pregnant but it wasn't yet showing. My daughter, the woman said, was very good at school and a very talented pianist, then she got a good law degree in the UK. My daughter married a successful lawyer last year, the woman said. It was noisy at the table so I had trouble understanding everything, and the aspiring mayor had started a conversation with the woman's daughter. Our conversations crossed. I leaned back and didn't have the impression I was listening to a nice story of a life well lived; instead, I felt the daughter's marriage was something like a knife, cutting the career out of her life. Or that there wasn't a caesura, that the career, as we call it, was something like a recipe experiment for the summer, something one had to have tried out before returning to regular recipes. I was very drunk that evening; I left without saying goodbye, swaying and not knowing where anything was heading.

At the kitchen table, I think about the most beautiful lady in the city, a woman of about seventy. She digs through the trash and wears clothes that are old but have come back into fashion now. She's ganglingly tall, hardly crooked. A moment ago she was twenty-five but age must have had a lightning-fast effect on her. Age grabbed hold of her and, unable to find anyone else at that moment, it made fast work of her toward the end—but she hasn't yet noticed. For the time being it's nothing but a kind of hangover, something like a confusing instant pain, a desolate matter that will soon show itself in full. She has a short blonde beard and wrinkles cast across her face in a chaotic pattern, having had no time to settle in convincingly. She stuffs a deposit bottle fished from a trashcan into her bag and moves on, her back only slightly bent.

I think of the old man who used to sit on an upturned bucket and sell flowers at various spots around town, who'd stammer that the flowers were all handpicked. At first his words were comprehensible; later I had to guess what he was saying. He'd sit all day and never grew older, as though he couldn't get any older than he already was. He always wore the same jacket made of parachute silk. I usually bought three bunches of flowers from him, but sometimes I evaded him and worried he might get beaten to death, or die of his own mental distress.

He'd sit there like a monument; I never saw him walking or standing.

I can't sit any more, though. I've got no more sitting power, nothing of the kind; I leap up every few minutes and walk around and sometimes I find respite in the thought of Robert Lax and his consoling question of why one should buy a bed when all that one wants is sleep.

So I really don't know what anyone can do to make something work out. Or I do know. I had the idea that you and I, whenever someone says *that's the way it is and that's the way it always will be*, whenever someone claims nothing ever really changes and never for the better, then you and I should both fall over backward together and start laughing. In my imagination, we have a subtle choreography of falling and laughing, and of course we often have to fall and laugh.

You do end up sleeping, and you wake up of your own accord ten minutes before your alarm. Unaccustomed to getting up early, you still don't waste any time. On the surface, everything goes perfectly well. You fill your thermos flask just before you leave, and you pack your sandwiches. You walk through the neighbors' sleep. Only a few smokers have their heads out of their windows, shivering or no longer noticing the cold. On the tram, you act blind. Where are you? Doesn't matter, you'd say. You're being driven to a destination, the most everyday act in the world. If only temporarily, you're enlisting into the ranks of working life much more clearly than before; this is a serious matter.

You look out into the darkness; on your right, the woman painted on the brothel by the water tower must be out there at some point, naïve, voluptuous, and joyful as ever. You miss her. You wish she'd get on your tram. When you get off you pause for a moment, and yes, it's possible to have skipped years and years, to forget everything and suddenly remember again. That you might disappear— that's what worries you.

But you're here. You're part of a group of workers. You're standing in line, not yet used to wearing your warning vest.

You hear shouts from the end of the line. You turn around. The tips of a bolt cutter protrude just above the employees' heads. The workers behind you move apart, making way for the bolt cutter, which you now see is being carried by the security woman. She's short, only as high as most people's shoulders, but she takes up a lot of space. She shouts: One of these days I'll end up killing one of you. Then the security woman presses against you from behind and you're pushed forward, and that makes you feel clearly that you're here, from beginning to end. You push back and the security woman takes a sidestep, alters her path, shoves past other employees. She's still holding the bolt cutter aloft like a tourist guide carries an umbrella.

You take your box off the shelf, stare at the list that Hans-Peter failed to find his name on, read your workstation number, and instantly forget it again. When Norman turns up he separates Hans-Peter off from the group. He says: You're needed elsewhere. Norman tells him to contact one of the leads, then he walks off with the rest of you and allocates you to your workplaces, which are no longer in the quieter corner of the hall but closer to the more practiced workers. One less problem, says Norman.

Next to you are crates of toys. Stuffed animals, rag dolls, not very memorable, the kind of faces you'd instantly forget if they weren't such a bright contrast to their surroundings. In this dusty workspace full of giant brown boxes and scuffed yellow totes, the animals and dolls look like garish ghosts, or as if someone had abducted them from a party and dragged them into the hall.

All the dolls and animals are packed in bags. There are many specimens of each stuffed animal, each doll. And each toy has a name, which it shares with all those it resembles down to the slightest detail. Their names are: My Friend Conny, Gildehard Günyburg, Mombel Wombel, and Möre Bröd. You're forced to look all of them in the face, against your will; you feel like you're at an event for identical sextuplets. You make an effort neither to chuck the toys around nor to lay them too carefully and tenderly in the tote.

You miscount; the computer beeps when you enter what you've counted. You count the items in the tote over again;

the computer beeps. You have to wait for the problem solver.

You say to Stefanie, working opposite you: I need someone like that quite often.

Stefanie says: I need him too, something's not right here.

The problem solver approaches slowly, pushing a tall desk on wheels ahead of him. He doesn't smile; none of the problem solvers will ever smile. None of them will ever even put on a friendly face. All problem solvers have had more than enough of problems and those who cause them, they all think of themselves as saviors waiting for a challenge rather than dealing day in, day out with banal difficulties caused by new workers. They act as though only their own kind might ever understand them.

The problem solver goes to Stefanie first, throws products out of her tote onto the desk, then holds up a toy doctor's kit, holds it right in front of Stefanie so she can see what she's forgotten to scan. He scans the barcode on the case, puts it in the tote and pushes his cart over to you. He checks the content of your tote, says you've put two Gildehard Günyburgs in the tote but only logged one in the system.

Scan them all separately, he says.

But, you say.

Scan them all separately, he repeats.

Later he comes back, dragging himself along again like a modern-day Sisyphus, for whom it would be easy to roll the stone up the mountain if only he weren't constantly interrupted by strangers' mistakes.

You say: I guess I counted wrong again.

Count better, he says. He takes all the products out of your tote, scans each one, and throws them on the desk. There's a dour look on his face.

Don't throw them, you say, sounding threatening.

But everyone counts wrong, it's annoying, says the problem solver. In the end he holds up Mombel Wombel, one too few of which was in the tote. You have to search through the cardboard boxes to try and find another Mombel Wombel. When you find one of the green rabbits, the problem solver throws it in the tote. You lift the tote onto the pallet, ready to be driven to the storage area once it's full. Only then do you see that the last Mombel Wombel does look very similar to the others but is actually smaller, and hence has been wrongly logged and hence will be wrongly dispatched. A small bunny will be sent out into the world with the product number of a big bunny. The problem solver is already dragging himself to his next case; no way do you want to bother him again.

Later, once your first independently logged pallet has been picked up by a forklift driver and you're waiting for Norman to come and tell you what to do, you sit down on the edge of a pallet. The soles of your feet are burning in your shoes. Up you get! calls a driver on his way past, but you ignore him, although it does occur to you that you're not allowed to sit on pallets, especially if there's no fiberboard on them. Part of this work is spending time with someone you wouldn't choose to spend time with. But that, you think, doesn't have to mean anything.

During your break, you peel the Band-Aids off your hands to apply new ones. You examine your hands for a moment. They're chapped and dirty; you'd like to go easier on them. You think of my father's hands, which were always dirty and rough. Two weeks' vacation were never enough to free them from all the dirt of working. To help loosen the dirt, he'd wash socks every weekend, dunking his hands in a pot of hand washing paste, taking a handful of the greasy, slightly grainy paste, applying it to the socks, rubbing them together, and then rinsing them. Stinging cuts would open up on his workingman's hands. They had pink spots, some of which were raw flesh, with leftover grey and black streaks. I'd always assumed he simply had hands like that; it had never occurred to me that those hands might have come about through his work.

You see now: you're getting workingwoman's hands.

Your new hands move goods, and your mind is a counting machine that keeps wandering. You do it well, nonetheless. You'll be informed of that in a few days' time and you won't have expected it at all. Some would say you just make things a bit hard for yourself. But the fact of the matter is you're standing next to a box of Italian model cars and realizing that the faux fancy packaging on most models is broken, the reflective foil has come loose and fallen on the cars, and some cars roll to and fro, no longer fixed in place. In other cases, the reflective foil is fogged over. What was intended to be the model car's showroom looks like a car dealership damaged by a storm and then never patched up.

You call the problem solver. It'll have to be the problem solver again, even though you don't want to call him. The problem solver says none of it matters as long as the product's OK, and it does seem to be.

You think for a while or you don't think at all, but you do stand around motionless and gaze at the large pile of cars with damaged packaging. In the end you hold up the boxes with loose and fogged-over foil and shake them to force the plastic back into its correct position. A futile undertaking, reflexive diligence; but you don't understand why you shouldn't put things into a respectable state. You open a few packages carefully and affix the reflective foil as best you can with a strip of tape. The pile barely decreases. You give up and receive the cars in the damaged packages as well, without repairing them first. You squint your eyes a little.

While you're working toward the end of your shift and you're tired and hungry and you count and count again all the time, and then count what you've counted all over again, I'm sitting in a café in town with a friend. We're chatting and drinking white wine spritzers; we haven't seen each other for a while. A very tall woman approaches our table, holding fliers fanned out in her hand, and asks whether we want to come along to a reading; it's starting in ten minutes. We shake our heads. No thanks, we say, we're leaving in a minute. As we pay our bill we spot the book that's about to be read from:

Monday at Last! The New Joy of Work Performance.

My friend says the book deserves an award for the worst title.

I start walking her to her hotel but we're not paying attention and we walk too far. She tells me about a hotel where she stayed a few years ago. It was actually a retirement home but they rented rooms to tourists when the city was booked up. My friend, expecting to find a hotel, hadn't noticed anything at first except a specific smell in her room, the smell of age, and it was only in the dining room in the midst of the old folks that she'd realized, firstly, that she must be in a retirement home, and, secondly, that the only vacant rooms in a retirement home were those where the occupants had recently died. The old people around her weren't travellers, then, she repeats, still not understanding how she'd failed to notice when she'd checked in. Maybe, she says, it was the hotel's name that distracted me. Avant-garde, she says—who'd guess it was a retirement home?

We do reach the hotel in the end, and you disembark from the tram at the station, exhausted. I come to collect you, still in a talking mood. I talk away at you, telling you about Hannah Arendt and how people come into the world as a beginning and that people have the ability for beginnings. Over and over again. You don't really listen to me but I go on talking and repeat what René Pollesch once said, that there has to be an end to these false activities "with which we pretend to treat each other humanely and as fellow human beings," and that we have to recognize, "if we notice nothing changes after a week," that we've chosen the wrong activity. "Then it has to stop, then we have to start something else that has a chance of changing something."

You look so tired and dusty. You say: That wouldn't work.

Perhaps I chose a bad moment. I walk a little slower, letting you walk ahead, and then I call out: What even works in the first place?

Six

You're actually doing fine.

You're doing pretty much like I did, a few years ago when I got a vacation job as a student, in the warehouse of a mail-order company that has since gone bust. I made an effort not to be too slow. But I didn't make an extraordinary effort. I needed the money but I wasn't desperate. I picked ordered products off shelves in the heated warehouse, I got lost among the shelves but I was still fast, and I stuck a label on every package so that the product would take the right route to the right customer later on, never sticking the label over the recycling information; that was forbidden. In the afternoons I met up with friends, or maybe I didn't. I bought heaps of peaches and fell asleep early. That's not much, but it's not nothing either. I knew all along that the job would have an end and, in any case, I had plans, a grand plan, in fact, for what lay ahead. In the second week, I missed my ride to the warehouse because my bus to the meeting point came late. One minute late. I stood on the marketplace and had no chance to get to the warehouse. I called but couldn't get hold of anyone. I took a bus back to my dorm, lay down in bed because nothing else occurred to me, slept briefly, had breakfast, and then, freshly recuperated, set out on the long journey to work. I apologized to my manager, who looked tired and smelled like he'd been partying all night. He nodded and I worked until my lunch break, and was then told to report to the glass managers' office. Who knows? I thought. Maybe I was even imagining a promotion. There were four women in housedresses in the office, and I took my place alongside them. We were a line that the manager, the whites of his eyes a deep shade of pink, had to get through. He fired each of us from left to right. He consulted his table, said something about work rate, and then said: We're going to let you go. To me, he said: You've attained very good scores. We're going to let you go. I said a great deal in my mind, but nothing in reality. I left the office, took a lunch break, then went back to my workplace, went on working, and had no idea why I didn't just stop and go home. I worked exactly like before, except I stuck the labels over the recycling instructions. It was nothing anyone would notice, but it was a big deal for me. I said not a word to myself or anyone else about having been fired. I got a job at a pizza place, chopping onions and making salads for five Deutschmarks an hour.

And you, if you please: have a little more patience. Things are about to get tough for you and you'll be shown a few boundaries that aren't your own actual boundaries, but they're the boundaries of the world in which you're the person right now whom I used to be. You'll soon have to slip into my role more fully; you won't be able to work it off on the side any more. So you'll be receiving, lugging products, and counting, counting at the same time as having to be me, a person who can't just let things go in one ear and out the other, can't learn to do that out of principle. You'll be so clearly in your role that I'd give you a round of applause, and maybe I will. Yeah, sure I will, and I'll applaud everyone who loses patience where patience has to be lost; in the words of Chris Köver, "You've probably noticed by now—the whole nonchalance thing doesn't quite kick it."

As a pragmatic early-shift person who has reported for the week and is now working that week off the way just about everything can be worked off, you stride through the dark morning, albeit shivering slightly, checking every clock you come across. What kind of time is this? It's a time when you direct almost your entire attention to the clock, but you haven't yet noticed that.

At any rate, it's time to put your locker key around your neck and fill your water bottle before your shift. You now do that routinely. You use the left-hand tap, and non-carbonated water runs into your bottle. A coworker joins you and uses the right-hand faucet, filling his bottle with sparkling water. He stands very close to you; that's how it is here. You press your right elbow against the man's belly but he doesn't even seem to notice. You press harder, your bottle now overflowing. Don't fall asleep, the man says, and closes the lid of his bottle. He didn't notice you woman-spreading at the tap. You laugh, take a big gulp from your bottle, and pass smoothly through the turnstile. You have a stride today that leads you almost above everyone's heads at speed, but you walk in their midst, and it's not down to you that a logjam forms down at the time clock; you've got your ID at the ready and you hold it up to the sensor as you pass. It's down to others who are newer than you, who have to examine what the screen says first, who wait for the display to formulate clearly that they've been logged in. You make small noises to express your annoyance, jostle a little, but you're not as snappy as those who pass by the waiting line and really hold their IDs up to the sensor as they walk, so fast that the new employee currently examining the screen and slowly raising his ID to the sensor doesn't even notice.

And now: things, oh boy, *things*. It's because of all the things that are here, which someone or another wants to buy, that you're here in the first place. Strange products in your hands, for example this baseball cap that already looks so lived-in it could hardly get much more worn. Used- or distressed-look fashion, you get the point, but the cap is nothing but a ragged piece of cloth, more like something for adherents to a radicalized acceleration of the commodity cycle, people who only buy what has to be thrown away because it fails to meet its requirements as a usable product, serves only to move money and material. The cap has an Iron Maiden logo on it and has slipped out of its bag. You almost sense the greasy feel of sweat mixed with dust. You're tempted to try it on for a moment, perhaps because it looks like something you found on the street for which you might have some use. A colleague at the next desk calls over that a guy was fired two weeks ago for trying out a skateboard he was supposed to be receiving. You nod, stuff the cap back in the bag, and tape it shut.

Many of the products you receive have travelled further than you have in the past five years. You're now processing mugs designed in Santa Monica, USA; made, printed, and packaged in China; then offered for sale in France; and now shipped from Amazon France to Amazon Germany as seasonal specials. A charity mug, the product description reads; the mugs boast self-portraits drawn by celebrities. You scan the barcode as usual and the computer reports the product has to go to the Sample Center because it hasn't yet been subjected to the drop test. So you take the mug in its cardboard packaging to the Sample Center. The associate there examines the box, stands up, and drops it on the floor from a height of a meter. He picks up the box and turns it so that a different corner will hit the floor first. You watch, fascinated. The man repeats the test. There's no clink of broken porcelain until the last drop. Well, the man says, no need to be too demanding—it's passed the test. He sniffles; he's got a cold. On his desk is an open plastic box containing two sandwiches, one of them with a bite taken out of it.

You're hungry too but you're not allowed to bring anything into the hall with you. You carry the mug back to your workplace, the well-travelled mug now clinking in shards inside its packaging.

You log the other mugs into the system and wonder who'll buy them, who'll buy all the other things. Surrounded by products you're preparing for sale, you don't get curious about things; you grow immune to them. You see the ridiculous side of reflexive consumption so clearly before you, and you're not like me, who once spent all the illicit cash I got paid—as the sole employee of a bad-tempered boss—almost the instant I earned it, buying all manner of things. I didn't like that boss but I never thought of quitting the job. The boss was always at risk of ending up in jail; he'd jump out of the window when creditors made an appearance, escaping across garage roofs. I had nothing to do except tell unexpected visitors and callers on the phone that he wasn't in the office, buy him four refrigerated minibottles of Prosecco a day from the shop on the corner—never all at once, only one after another throughout the day—and wait eight and a half hours a day for the one and only letter to be typed. I was bored, until I began writing my first book right under my boss's nose, which helped slightly. After work I had to get rid of the cash. I could have given it to charity but I had to convert it into things I didn't need but wanted to own, things that didn't suit me.

If someone asked you what you need right now, you might say: Seeing as I really needed a job, or more precisely money, I won't complain now that my first payday's approaching. I'll soon have what I need.

And I'll say, in a questioning tone, in the words of Friederike Mayröcker:

> you need a tree you need a house
> not one all for you just a corner a roof
> to sit under to think to sleep to dream

Sure, you say, but strictly speaking that's not actually enough. And you're right, I'm sure.

You look closely at the mugs with the self-portraits of George Clooney, Madonna, Robbie Williams, and so on, and put them slowly into the tote. It's very easy to explain why these mugs exist, why they travel the world and get bought or are supposed to get bought. But each one of these mugs and most of the other products are really dull as soon as you take a look; it doesn't have to be that close a look.

Later on, you'll start to like things again, the way I do now. You'll like fewer things than before, but you'll still buy them or want to buy them. Yes, you like money. The money you have or ought to have. For the time being, though, you sit down on a pallet for a moment and gaze at the pallet next to you, stacked up with wheeled children's toys that are all sorts of things at once: a chair for pushing along, a kind of balance bike, and a car. You wait a little before you log these products in, and you suspect this: that the superego is a thing made up of things.

Next to you is your task before the lunch break, a crate so huge it makes you laugh and cry, a crate that makes you look like a tiny little human being, one that has received a sumptuous gift and has to stand on tiptoe to open it. You use your cutter to remove the lid flaps, which are as bulky as window shutters. Inside the box are red plastic cases: children's emergency sets for rescuing boring clothes, including a children's cellphone. According to the picture, the case contains sequins, stickers, bows, and a figurine for trying out all the emergency clothing-rescue measures.

Everything exists, in case you were going to ask. Absolutely everything exists, and people can buy it all.

After washing your hands, you join the line in the cafeteria and get a plate of soothingly overcooked pasta with sausage and tomato sauce. You're already eating much faster than at the beginning of your seasonal job. One might say you shovel your food down. You've eaten half your meal when Stefanie and Grit join you and unwrap the sandwiches they've brought in, scrunching up the aluminum foil into little balls. Have they seen Hans-Peter around? No, they say. Stefanie's heard he's working the garbage compactor now, but she doesn't know for sure. Who knows? you say and go on chewing. A lot of food fits in your stomach. While your generously filled plate empties, you peer over at the food your workmates are carrying from the counter to the tables. Stefanie and Grit get up to go for a cigarette and ask you to keep an eye on their bottles and the rest of their provisions. When the two of them aren't back after five minutes, you stand up, take your plate to the dirty-dish counter, and leave the cafeteria. No one has all the time in the world, but anyone with only a half-hour break that includes the walk to the break area and the walk back to their workplace has too little time to spend it on waiting.

You replace the Band-Aids on your hands. Your thumbs, forefingers, and middle fingers on both hands now have hangnails from all the reaching into totes and boxes and from cutting and folding cardboard. Harmless irritations, but they make every movement harder. You hear the words *shift termination*, although nobody uses them, and you look around. Oh, you think, interesting. And of course, there's a wish implanted in your mind: May every day be a day when shifts are terminated, ideally right after they begin. Before you get back to work you go to the restroom, and that's just the beginning of a retreat, a partial entering of the restroom, which will soon seem to you like a place that belongs at least a tiny bit to you, here in this gigantic hall. A place that's not transparent, where no one checks on you, where it's quiet and the light's not too bright. A place comparable to your employee box, where you now keep rushed notes on yellow Post-its along with your Band-Aids, hair bands, and candies. In case you don't already write, the dispatch hall is a good place to start writing. Pretty much the best place. You need to be rescued, if not now then soon.

Until then, though, you receive tool kits so heavy you shouldn't be allowed to move them on your own. You receive aquariums and luminous globes; you know the ropes now. Although you don't yet know everything about this work, you do know enough to do it well. You've internalized the procedures. Unfortunately, there's no next useful lesson to learn, you can't flick forward to a new chapter offering you fresh, interesting material. You remain on this level and you look around; presumably everyone here does. It's all about sheer endurance, about presence, about translating your time and energy into money.

So while you're thinking you now have everything in the bag and all you have to do is mark off the days, an experience is preparing itself, a minor intermezzo I'd have gladly done without. But I'll still share it with you:

Next to your workplace is a pallet for cubi-totes. Products that are new in the warehouse and haven't yet been measured go in what's called a cubi-tote, which is taken on a pallet to one of several cubi-tote collection points. If one collection point is full, you look for another one. Near the end of each shift, the pallets of cubi-totes are collected and taken for measuring. There's a pallet like that next to your workplace, very full of cubi-totes, stacked above the maximum level. Leaning towers beside you, which also wobble because the bottom layer consists not of totes, but of cardboard boxes, which can't take the weight of the crates piled on top of them. A punching bag is propped up against the already unstable totes. You adjusted the punching bag in the morning so it wouldn't fall over and bring everything crashing down with it, and you do the same now. Along comes a coworker with a cubi-tote from somewhere on your left, and stacks it on top of one of the wobbly towers. You say: It's going to fall over.

He dismisses you with a waving gesture and says: No one cares anyway.

You say: I care.

That gesture again, and he turns to leave. You instantly lose your temper. Attempting to keep your voice calm, you ask him to stow his tote safely or, better still, somewhere else. If it falls over, you say, it'll be my feet it falls on. Your coworker looks at you as though you were at the end of a long tunnel, as though he had to adjust his focus to even see you.

I can't do it any better, he says, the pallet's full.

Take it to another one then, you say.

I don't get paid for long walks, he says, and leaves.

You watch him go and you take your time, you have to slow down right now, although or in fact because you feel like running after him, fetching him back so he'll take his tote away again. He's beating a retreat, he's simply leaving, you think. His pants are hanging loose, dusty gray on the seat, and the contours of an undershirt show through his T-shirt. You're presumably tempted right now to repeat the man's dismissive gesture, but you're me so that's out of the question. You take his tote—containing a child's alarm clock, a thermos flask, and a disposable camera—and you carry it toward him with powerful strides. You say: Here, take it. You want everything to be clear now, clearer than clear.

He says: Are you kidding me? You turn away and walk across the hall with the tote to look for a place for it. Your hands are trembling; you're ashamed of yourself.

You can't back down now, though. You empty the pallet next to your workplace, rearrange it. Totes at the bottom, cardboard boxes on top. You drag the punching bag to another cubi-tote pallet, which is empty but well hidden. There's no more wobbling now. You go back to receiving— silver kitchen implements, you don't look that closely— you're still trembling, still agitated, when the man comes up to you without you noticing.

You didn't really rearrange it, did you? he asks.

Now it won't fall over, you say.

The man does a facepalm. You fix your eyes on the strand of hair now stuck to his forehead from the force of his hand.

You must have a screw loose, he says.

You give him with a questioning look.

He repeats that you must have something wrong with you.

And then you yell at him: Get out of here, get out of my face.

He's on your turf; you're taking possession of a zone for yourself because you need one right now. For this moment, this workplace in the darker, quieter part of the dispatch hall belongs to you. Your coworker pauses for an instant, then shakes his head, and leaves.

You're involved in a matter that might be easier to solve if you had intercultural communication skills.

You're like a coal miner who wants to split a rock with a big heavy hammer, who raises a hammer he can hardly lift, and brings the hammer down on the rock with full force, but can't make even the tiniest chink. You hope for fast results, where only continuous light work is possible and necessary on that rock.

You receive cheese graters, miscounting three times in a row.

You take a walk and hide in the bathroom. There, you don't cry the internalized tears of more experienced employees; you cry internally and externally at the same time.

After a while you calm down and ask yourself what just happened. What a commotion, you think, and this is what you decide: Deal with it like the hero of a courtly romance who fails at the first attempt. You have to ride out once again and act more wisely this time.

You return to your workplace, where the full cubi-tote pallet has meanwhile been replaced by an empty one, and you too want to go back to a beginning. You notice the guy watching you, as well as anyone can watch someone out of their corner of their eye. You stride over to him. He straightens up.

You say: I'd like to apologize. I didn't mean to shout. I apologize for shouting at you.

The man lets you finish. Then he says: Did you really lug that punching bag halfway across the hall?

You shrug.

Your coworker says: That punching bag went with the parts in the boxes. It was one product. You broke one product down into parts, and now no one can put it together again. You caused total chaos.

He does that gesture again.

You blush and say: But if you saw that and knew it was wrong, you could have told me and then I wouldn't have done it.

He says: There was no talking to you.

Yes, there was, you think, and I agree with you, you're

easy enough to talk to. People can always talk to you, no matter how you seem; you're a receptive person, it's just you're not receptive to ignorance.

You say nothing, just stand and stare, majorly uprighting your posture so that you don't collapse in front of him or lose your temper again.

The man says: The cubi guys will have a whole lot of problems, they'll be looking for all the parts.

You say: Anyway, I wanted to apologize for shouting at you.

You turn away and leave. You feel totally vulnerable, unable to protect yourself from him.

Don't show weakness, you think. Don't show any weakness in front of him. Don't show any weakness in front of anyone here. But what is weakness and what isn't? You fetch a sheet of fiberboard from a pile in the corner and drag it after you. You're a tired old sheep now, seeing all meaning in its tiredness and having to make space for that meaning. You put the board down on the pallet, sit down, and think: I'm showing weakness. I'm showing weakness and I'm allowing myself weakness. You don't understand yourself.

You lie down on the pallet. If someone asked, you'd say you were feeling a little nauseous. You stare up at the day-light lamps, fill your eyes with the cool light, and let the pattern that appears when you close your eyes—a little purple crescent—wander across the ceiling.

Your dream job right now: industrial spy without an espionage mission—present, of no account, walking the aisles of Amazon.

Here are a few employee phrases:

Don't take it to heart.
Just grit your teeth and get through it.
Some things you just have to put up with.
Don't be such a wimp.
It's all a load of crap.
Another fine mess the top dogs have come up with.
Once I've won the lottery you won't see me for dust.

After your shift, you stand at the tram stop in the last grains of daylight, walking large circles around your waiting workmates. The sun will be setting any minute now; the shortest day of the year hasn't come yet. The trams run from right to left, from the city center to the edge of town. None come from the edge of town, though.

Where to go? Out of here!

You set off, ready to walk all the way into town or wherever your feet take you. You've hardly started walking when the trams start running again. You wait at the next stop, letting one tram pass because it's so crowded.

The next tram is empty. You take your thermos out of your bag and drink tea with your legs drawn up, propped against the seat in front. Five young men in white work pants get on the tram, sit down near you and act out a scene, an after-work scene made up of these men and a woman within earshot and sight of them. One of them is a childlike-looking man with glasses, perhaps with a learning disability, who laughs at everything the others say to him.

The men say to the glasses guy:

Oh give us a blow job.
Yeah go down on me.
Get her wet, she's really into you.
Blow me.
You're gay.
No you're gay.
Dong.
Long dong.
Longest dong.
Zero dong.
Hot chick.

You think: I'm going to whack them over the head with my thermos flask. You sit there, outwardly calm with your eyes closed, but in fact you're just about to beat them over the heads with your thermos.

And you're absolutely right. As Chris Köver, again, says: "… the healthy reaction to all these circumstances isn't coolness, it's anger. A really deep state of being thoroughly pissed. Anger is something women aren't often granted; it distorts our pretty faces and doesn't come across as all that docile. Anger is excellent though for transforming into the energy we need to act against the things that trigger that anger."

That's how it is: you're exhausted now, not just physically; your mind, which is also a little bit your heart, has sustained damage as well. Or your heart, which is also a little bit your mind, has sustained damage.

And I didn't even give you a round of applause, I realize, when it was most necessary. I just forgot.

Seven

Early evening. You find yourself sitting in an uncomfortable position on a kitchen chair. Waiting for the water to boil for your tea after work, you nodded off in the kitchen; sleep caught up with you but didn't take good care of you. Your reflection in the windowpane shows a shiny forehead and small, reddened eyes, beneath them dark circles and burning cheeks. Opposite, in the meeting room of PricewaterhouseCoopers, people are preparing for an office Christmas party; you watch them, incapable of moving. All you can do is stand and shiver, eventually fetching a thermometer. You register with amazement that you're running a pretty high fever. You get into bed. I bring you your tea. You're trembling so I bring you all the blankets I can find. I know what to do when someone's sick. I wrap lukewarm damp cloths around your calves, not too cold. You fall straight to sleep; you're a heavy weight on the bed, almost a burden upon it. At PricewaterhouseCoopers opposite, employees stroll in conversation through the brightly lit space. One of them sits at a table next to a whiteboard, his legs stretched out and his feet resting on the table. A woman ladles mulled wine out of a large pan. They've all rolled up their sleeves. But you don't see that. You're asleep in your bed, which isn't Tracey Emin's bed now, it's a clean and tidy and freshly sheeted bed for an invalid; you sweat and freeze at the same time.

Being rarely sick, not the slightest bit interested in being sick, I think of a man I know, a psychotherapist who presented a simple equation: When he's sick he returns to health either quickly or slowly, depending on the work he has to do over the next few days. If he has to go to the hospital where he's employed as a therapist, he's generally sick for an average of four days and goes back to work with a cough. If he wants to go to his own practice, though, to work with patients only he works with, meaning he doesn't have to accept treatment plans and go through with them without discussion, all he usually needs is one night of good, deep sleep. The next day, he can continue his work, still coughing but otherwise barely affected. Sometimes, he says, he can get an illness out of the way overnight, and sometimes he can't, and he says he finds it interesting, at least, and hopes he can soon make a living out of his own practice.

When you wake up in the middle of the night, the fever's gone.

I can tell you're wondering where in the world the sickness has gone. It won't just have pulled an all-nighter on you? It won't have crept off without leaving anything behind so you'll have to go to work, recovered far too quickly? But I can reassure you: You have aching limbs and an inflamed throat. You have a headache and a cough too. Anyone can see and hear that you're sick.

You kneel on the bed and peer through the bare branches of the plane tree in the backyard. An infant is crying somewhere and one of the day's first trams is passing, further away. At PricewaterhouseCoopers, where it was dark until a moment ago, the lights in the second-floor corridor go on. A cleaning woman enters an office, the tube lights flicker, the cleaning woman makes fast work of her job, empties the wastepaper baskets into a wheeled container in the corridor, takes a brief, routine look around, switches off the light, closes the door, and moves on to the next room, which is the meeting room. There, she pauses and seems not to know: Is it part of her job to clean up the remains of the party, to make the room look like the party never took place? Or does she only have to empty the wastepaper baskets and clean the whiteboard, as usual? If she cleans up the meeting room she'll get out of her rhythm, she won't manage to clean the other rooms by six o'clock, there'll be work left over. This cleaning woman— you see this much—is a determined one. After a brief tour of the room, a quick dip into a bowl presumably containing potato chips, she does no more than usual, the un–cleared up party like water off a duck's back to her.

I've had a lot of jobs, and maybe you have too. In any case, you've got my seasonal associate job at Amazon, which is more than sufficient to find out everything a person can find out about the working world in its most common form.

You pass the time until 5:30 with reading. Then you have to call your boss and tell him you're sick. Your eyes dart across the same lines over and over, absolutely unaffected, running up and down these sentences written by Eva Meyer: "When space gets too crowded it's time to sidestep to time … So imagine we could overcome that boundary in a chrono-political sense and activate its non-contemporary and non-redeemed aspects in the cohabitation of time, instead of co-opting it in the geopolitical sense." You don't understand, but later you'll begin to understand what you're reading now, once it's almost time for you to be no longer me but whoever you are again.

Across the street, the man from the security firm and the cleaning woman cross paths, apparently not saying hello even though they've seen each other every morning for the past two years.

You reach for the phone, fearfully steeling yourself to be immediately fired. You have your preconceptions about companies you work for. You think defiant thoughts: I'll just look for a new job if they fire me. Let me tell you what you already know—you won't find a new job that fast and that easily, you'd presumably have to dream up a job to be found in a short time and put it on the floor in front of you so that you could trip over it and take the job and it wouldn't go to someone else who happens to be closer and grabs the job you've invented faster than you do.

You dial the number printed on one of the cards you wear on a lanyard along with your employee ID badge. You hope for an answering machine but Mirko picks up the phone in person. You say: I'm afraid I can't come, I've got a bad cold. I can tell by your voice that you're sick, says Mirko. Get well soon—call when you're ready to work again.

Your supervisor's friendliness wins you over to the whole company; you're so relieved, you look forward to going back to work and you almost take it as praise that they didn't fire you on the spot.

I read in Lafargue: "A strange delusion possesses the working classes of the nations where capitalist civilization holds its sway. This delusion drags in its train the individual and social woes which for two centuries have tortured sad humanity. This delusion is the love of work, the furious passion for work, pushed even to the exhaustion of the vital force of the individual and his progeny." Presumably, though, no one really has a furious passion for work, and Lafargue knew that too. You're certainly not possessed by any delusionary passion for work at the moment. You're now sleeping in an almost cheerful frame of mind.

I work, though, and I can't quite tell any more whether my work is *labor*, whether I want to call it that. I work a lot, I think, so that I don't have to go to work, to the place where the working world is the way it is, and is changing far too slowly. I think of Gertrude Stein, who liked to sit in the bathtub and kick her legs and stamp her feet, which we could view at least as a prerequisite for her work. A while ago, I asked at the video store about films on the subject of work. Andrea, the video store owner, went through the shelves by the counter where she keeps the documentaries. Right, she said, there's *Workingman's Death* or Michael Moore's films; or *The Whisperers*, about interpreters; or *Cinemania*, about New York movie buffs who can't stop going to the cinema, they learn the listings by heart, come up with plans and routes so as not to miss one movie, not one beginning of one movie. That's work too, Andrea said. And you can certainly see it like that.

So I work or I don't work, doing both with a sense of urgency, though, in a hurry and for many hours of almost every day, because I'm afraid—but I only say this to my closest friends—of getting tired again if I sleep too much, falling into hesitation and procrastination or back into that situation where I really had no money and didn't know where to find the entrance to the world. So I'm always semisleepless and I know a lot of people like that. Lafargue asks: "Where are those neighborly housewives told of in our fables and in our old tales, bold and frank of speech, lovers of Bacchus. Where are those buxom girls, always on the move, always cooking, always singing, always spreading life, engendering life's joy, giving painless birth to healthy and vigorous children?" And I say: Oh, they're still around, they're me and this or that friend of mine, we can do all that, we can be those neighborly women. We can't always do it, but we can do it, we can be on the move and party and drink and smoke like crazy and survive the next weekday with TV shows, with entire seasons of TV shows, or we can be more moderate about it, and we don't always want to spread life, we've presumably spread enough life already and certainly didn't give painless birth—in other words, sometimes we can be the best, most exemplary neighborly housewives, part-time neighborly housewives, because no one can keep it up forever. Apart from Jens, my restless friend Jens, always on the move with a giggle on his lips and a lot of luggage in one hand and a beer in the other and a word for everyone, Jens who knows everything, knows everything in his own way and brings gifts for everyone he likes—things he finds lying around in the street like cauliflowers or skis—who distributes his gifts with thought, who sometimes decorates potted plants with gummy bears, then laughs and falls over and lies on his back like a drunk but happy bug, apparently unable to believe his luck. With a guy like that, I say, we could fall too; with a guy like Jens we could perfect the art of falling over backward.

As a seasonal associate, you're not raring to go out and party, you don't want to crawl from one bar to the next, all you're lacking is an unblocked view of the days, the rest of the year that seems not to belong to you any more. You consider how expandable your illness is. Setting Lafargue aside, I think of a workmate I used to have. She was always wearing new clothes; I rarely saw the same item on her twice. I read on one of her T-shirts: *I am crazy! I am free!* Being a person who reads everything, I read over and over what it said across her breasts and her belly, and I thought: That's just not true. She used to sit opposite me, giggling a lot but complaining even more. She'd stick loyalty points from packs of coffee onto a sheet of paper; she'd collected more than fifty of them. That was the advantage of having to buy the coffee, a task that was otherwise just another nuisance to her—she was entitled to all the loyalty points and she exchanged them later on, exchanged points for mugs, and it seemed to me that was more of a reward to her or a better reward than the wages she received punctually every month as a long-term employee, usually with a bonus on top. She said to me: I have to open that file cabinet and lock it again so often!

Twice a day, I said, but she didn't hear.

It's not good for my back, she said. I looked at her body, the seated body that she left seated in her breaks as well, and I knew she'd soon call in sick again and tell a long story on the phone in the morning, only to say how everything was related to everything and how it was absolutely inevitable that she now had stomach problems too.

You've forgotten your minor morning joy over not getting fired; you're annoyed that you now have to go to a doctor. Seeing as you've never been required to provide evidence of illnesses, you don't have a family doctor. You do some research and decide on a nearby medical practice. You pause for a moment, inspecting yourself—yes, you're still sick.

You walk into the practice just before ten. Sounds of coughing emanate from the waiting room. Hello, you say, and no one answers. After a little while, during which you locate your insurance card, the receptionist looks up at you. I'm sick, you announce, because you can't think of anything better to say. You hand over your insurance card, unpracticed and wondering whether you have to say right away that you've come for a sick note, whether one has to inform the doctor in advance.

You're told to take a seat in the waiting room. The air there is stuffy. A quarter of the room is taken up by a jardinière, the leaves of its Mediterranean plants growing out toward the waiting patients' heads; there's a table holding glasses and a bottle of water. The glasses are stacked with their bottoms up, coated in a thin layer of dust. The room has a patina of sickness; you drape your scarf over your nose and mouth. To your left, an old woman with guttural breathing is reading a pharmacy magazine. Everyone in the waiting room looks up when a new patient walks in; only a few of them say hello.

The old woman stands up and opens a window. A young woman is sitting next to the window. She has a heavy cough and is sniffling, wearing an anorak but apparently still cold. You take greedy breaths of the fresh air, stretching your head out to get as much of it as you can. The woman in the anorak begins to murmur, complaining quietly but clearly about the older woman. And I've been waiting so long, she says. It's ridiculous, says the man she's with. He gets up and slams the window shut. The old woman shakes her head, now murmuring herself. This, you think, is how wars are started, and I think of a strike at Amazon that I went to take a look at, to see what was going on, feeling connected to the strikers even though my seasonal job was long over by that point. On the way from the tram stop I passed about ten porta-potties in a row—great plans seemed to be afoot. But all I found was a scattered, elongated crowd of people, which I passed with a nervous smile as I kept an eye out for familiar faces in the midst of this calm, apparently unthreatening picket line. I wanted to buy a coffee but I got it for free.

I spoke to a man who looked approachable; he was eating a hot sausage. I asked how the strike was going; he chewed. Oh sorry, I said.

Well, he said, wiping his mouth on a paper napkin, there's a few of us but it could be better. There are talks going on and we've achieved a couple of things, but we still want to be paid in line with the retail wage agreement.

I told him I'd worked there as a seasonal associate. He said he used to be a teacher but he didn't want to do it any more after the Wall came down. The parents had too many questions, they were suddenly always wanting something from me, I didn't like it any more.

I said: Amazon always paid on time, that surprised me.

Yes, he said. A lot of things are fine here, but no one reports about that.

I wanted to relativize that but I didn't.

He said: Maybe we'll see each other again, maybe you'll have a chance to work here again.

I said: Oh, I have enough work, it was just for a while when I really needed the money.

He said: They're often looking for people, maybe it'll work out.

I said: Well, yeah, maybe, and then I said goodbye.

A few weeks later when they were back on strike, I heard about the T-shirts worn by the workers who weren't striking: *We love Amazon.* A clear commitment to their employer, implying that only those who weren't striking valued their employer. What a misunderstanding, I thought, to blame the strikers for a new dispatch facility in Eastern Europe taking the place of this one earlier than planned, to accuse them of endangering the entire facility, hence their own jobs and those of their co-workers. I thought: What annoying nonsense. I thought:

What a shame; there's always a little bit of war everywhere you look.

Back in the waiting room, the young woman is still complaining. You close your eyes and sit in an ocean of time, as though you'd been working at Amazon for years; you feel as if you'd mastered a really large workload. Your internal screenwriter demands a big closing scene, but none comes and it never will. No grand gesture, nothing that might be good for a minor showdown. Only thoughts, which go far but not far enough, and nothing that would now—or then, when you end your time as a seasonal associate with absolute consistency—be recognizable on a screen.

The old woman next to you hears her name being called and walks out, with a crooked gait. When's it my turn? the young woman asks, trembling. I'll go and have a word, says the man with her, and he stands up. No, don't, she says. He goes to the counter anyway: How much longer do we have to wait?

People who accompany other people to the doctor, you think sleepily, and then stop thinking. You look at the young man who's just come in. It's me again, he says, for my blood test. Yes, says the receptionist, you've been in a few times. Let's have a try. Not the end of the world if it goes wrong, is it? The nurse leads the patient over to the bathroom, brings him a chair, asks him to sit down, and turns on the water. You don't understand exactly what's going on.

Your name is called and you automatically assume a facial expression of slight suffering. You enter the consultation room, stopping briefly next to the doctor writing at her desk, and continuing when she doesn't look up. You sit down opposite the doctor and cough a ridiculous cough, which was genuine until a moment ago and will be genuine again afterward. You feel like you're faking. How dare it— you grow enraged in your thoughts—how dare your employer intervene in your nice private sickness, how dare it prompt you to suspect you're not ill at all, that you just want to get out of working so as to harm them. However, because in this case I know better, I say: It's not your current employer that's unnerving you here, it's more the after-effects of my mother's first and for a long time only employer, the East German Post Office, which made total and utter use of my mother and never allowed her a break, which meant my mother was always rather glad when I was ill because it was easier to stay home from work when she had a sick child. I'm not saying my mother hoped I'd get at least a minor, sufficiently convincing illness, but I am saying she didn't swear silently like I do now when my children are sick and I can't get to my desk, or barely can. And I know too: sometimes I wasn't sick, sometimes I just pretended, and my mother gave me advice on how to look and what to say if we ran into any of her workmates. So it's that childhood playacting that's making you assume you might be putting on an act now.

While the doctor goes on making notes, let me tell you a little more about my mother, who started work at the age of fourteen, and now knows all about leaving the working world. She often used to say: You just act a bit crazy and they'll send you off to early retirement. But I can't do that. If only I could.

A while ago, I accompanied my mother to a court hearing. Arthritic and released into early retirement, my mother had to go to court against the pensions office. They wanted to see my mother working again, but my mother couldn't and wouldn't work another day.

Essentially, my mother wasn't work-shy; she was the opposite of work-shy, more an excessively conscientious person who took on all work, which is why work had managed to cause the greatest and clearest damage to her and eventually turned her into a person who needed to escape work.

My mother wore simple everyday clothes to the court hearing; she'd been advised not to dress up, to look poor but not like she neglected her appearance. Her lawyer smelled like a smoke-filled room and my mother wanted nothing to do with him. She'd have preferred the pensions office lawyer, who sat at his table with a fat binder and had many other cases ahead of him.

The judge, a mild-looking, polite person, asked how long my mother had taken to walk from the station to the court, and my mother said twenty minutes, but she'd had to lean on a bollard for a five-minute rest. Despite my mother's actual infirmity, which has never been doubted, a performance took place that day, beginning even before she arrived at court. She had left the house at a slower pace than usual and then left the train bravely with her constantly painful knee, smiling as she walked and trying to look composed. She knew the rule that said she must not be able to walk longer than fifteen minutes in one go, if she was to stay in early retirement.

How would my mother have walked if she hadn't been appearing in court and hadn't had to consider that rule? In the same way, except it would mainly have been internal. On the outside, my mother would have concentrated on pointing out trip hazards and people pushing and shoving, or she'd have looked out for a café and said: I could sit in the sun watching people for hours.

I'd been in court as my mother's audience and companion. The judge had come in with his robe wafting in the draft and the play had begun. My mother provided her reports, describing how her knee was a handicap and wouldn't improve.

The judge suggested that my mother—who, on close examination of the case and the labor market, wouldn't be able to work any more anyway—should be released into permanent retirement. That earned him the ire of both lawyers; they hadn't yet fought their main battle and felt cheated out of combat. The pensions office lawyer said she could work perfectly well, and could be expected to carry out light, seated activities for ten hours a week. My mother's lawyer said the other lawyer ought to give her that activity, if such a thing existed. His opponent responded that he might well do that. They agreed on a further extension of the temporary retirement status, with the next hearing in three years' time.

My mother stood up after the verdict, only to sit straight back down again. In the end she limped out of the court on weak knees, no longer knowing how strongly she was actually limping.

I think of Heinrich Böll, of his novel *Group Portrait with Lady* and the leg he describes in it, allegedly the most dishonest leg in the world. I think a dishonest leg is better than one that's actually diseased; under all circumstances, it makes sense to stick out a dishonest leg to trip up this working world that you'll have to be part of for a little while longer. There's no point in talking to it.

The doctor does stand up for a moment, in the end, and looks at you. Hours might have passed. What's the problem? she asks, and opens a new patient file, presumably yours. You explain that you had a fever during the night, that everything's hurting and you can't go to work. Where do you work? the doctor asks. At Amazon in the warehouse, you say. It's heavy physical work. Yes, say the doctor and looks up briefly and firmly. Work is hard. Yes, you say, to emphasize that you know that. You're really in a test, in a job interview for a sick note. After this slight false start that must have made you look work-shy, you have to show that your sickness exists and you're essentially willing to work, merely prevented from doing so at the moment. I just need a little break, I've caught a chill, you say. It's so cold there. My hand's hurting too but it'll be fine after a break.

Break or sick? asks the doctor. That's two different things.

Both, you say.

This is an army examination in which your body is not under scrutiny. The doctor makes plenty of notes but doesn't listen to your lungs or look at your throat. Are you sure you want to go back to work again after the break? the doctor asks. You focus on a portrait of a young woman on the right-hand side of the desk, wondering whether she's the doctor's daughter or partner. You'd like to say: Forget it! I don't want your sick note! For understandable reasons, this doctor has no wish to issue one note after another, operating a sick note–issuing racket, to be a sickness certifier rather than a doctor, but instead you nod. Yes of course, you say. I'm just sick.

Later, you take your sick note to the mail. You're running a fever again and you wish you were in bed, lying down in it the instant you get home. Your bed is the best home and it could be that way forever. Without giving yourself a specific account of it, you suddenly understand the cocooning phenomenon, albeit not for long, and you also understand ambitious all-day home-cooking sessions, collecting travel catalogs, dreaming of the future, upgrading home interiors, wallpapering with soft carpets, you understand blankets with arm holes, fur-lined slippers, housecoats, morning home clothing, noon home clothing, evening home clothing, reading circles, corner sofas, evenings in front of the TV.

You hide yourself away—in the meantime, I'm getting off a train in Munich. While I sent you to the doctor I embarked on a trip, and I'm not sure whether it's a work trip or a personal one. I needed a trip, so I'm going on a trip, and now I'm walking around Munich, admiring my reflection in the windows of Fendi and Prada and Luis Vuitton, and I can't afford anything I see in those windows but that doesn't bother me, hardly at all.

Above me is the best Munich sky; yours has been dark for hours now. In the apartment below you, a man laughs loudly like he does at this time every day. Then he yawns several times, almost certainly with his mouth wide open, and after that there's no sound of him. Instead, the radiators hiss, hissing all the way to your stomach. You put your hands over your ears—that sound is enough to make you lose your mind. You turn the radiators off and the sound only gets louder and fills the whole apartment.

I'm sitting in a beer garden, under a tree labeled Chestnut #13. I could stay here, I think, I could write everything I have left to write in one go here, I could sit here until I'm weather-beaten, at least every day until closing time, I'd like my own mailbox here so the best mail would reach me at the address Chestnut #13.

I order *leberkäse*, a pretzel, a blackcurrant soda; the waiter repeats everything. Happy to serve you, he says after that. Happy to serve me? I turn it into a question, and I laugh.

Behind me, a group of American tourists empties two full glasses underneath the table because flies landed in their drinks. Basking in the sun, I'm waiting for a woman I've worked with once before and hope to work with again. She will tell me about the man she can no longer trust, and about the other man whom she loves, and I'll say: Oh, I could just cry. And she'll say calmly: Go ahead and cry. Which will impress me, because most people would say: No, don't cry! We'll move from the personal to the professional and we'll know where one stops and the other begins, but we won't have to separate them at all times. Until she arrives, though, I eat greedily and read Mónica de la Torre, whose book I've brought along on my little trip because she's clever. She writes:

My economy is broken, mispronounced.
My economy has cold feet, even if there are plenty
    of socks at home.

My economy would like to be wholesome and
sound.

My economy is a gift certificate that is not enough
for what I'd like to have, so I end up spending
money at a store that I dislike in the first place
and will never visit again.

My economy is a business lunch where I end up
paying the bill instead of the person who'd like
me to work with her.

My economy consists of performing tasks for which
I receive no quantifiable pay.

My economy grows when it's enough to buy someone else a drink, or a meal.

My economy does not allow me to say no.

My own little economy is still my favorite but I wouldn't
tell you that now—or, in fact I am telling you, because
why should I go easy on you? I whisper into your sleepy head
how great my economy is and how fully comprehensible
that you're trying to avoid yours, the current and foreseeable
seasonal economy.

You sleep a heavy sleep and awake in the morning with
days to count down. How many days you still have off sick
(three); how many days you'll still have to work after the
sickness (twenty-one). You have to make a move now—
you could use an airplane that takes several hours to fly
you somewhere, but you make do with a stroll through
the city center.

You watch the fire brigade putting up a Christmas tree near the entrance to the new city tunnel. The tree was donated by a local family; it had to be felled anyway, the family is quoted in the local newspaper, it was too tall and too slanting for their small front garden and its roots had begun lifting the paving stones outside. Once the tree is erect, technicians begin attaching the lights, a task that will take hours.

At the other end of the market, forklifts are transporting halves of wooden holiday market stands, lifting them from a row of parked delivery trucks. In mid-air, the floors of the huts wobble and bend and reveal their insides: wall cabinets, sink constructions, presentation shelves. The wooden walls don't emit a single creak, and nothing splinters or breaks as the huts are set down.

You walk as though through a vacuum, making frequent stops, eating overly spicy food in a Vietnamese place, so hot your face breaks out in a sweat. You're hoping for a business idea you can put into practice; you're under time pressure. You need something you can develop by the end of your sick leave so that you'll have a good justification for yourself if you quit your seasonal job prematurely. You can't think of anything at all. Then you think, and you think it very slowly: welfare. Right, welfare, why not? You picture a simplified life for yourself. You tell yourself: The regular payments will calm my nerves. My nerves need calming.

You're wrong, you're very wrong. While I'm waiting for the beginning of *Orpheus Descending* at the Munich Kammerspiele Theater, about to forget you temporarily, let me shout out to you that it would be nothing but sedation, at most a partial anesthesia, it would only help for a moment and in addition—whether you're listening or not—you have to bear in mind what all anesthetists know: even a general anesthetic is no protection from the phenomenon of awareness, which occurs more frequently than reported. I swear to you, and I never usually swear, that that calming measure would be putative and it would backfire. You'd still be aware of everything. And you'd know precisely what you're trying to avoid, and that you really have to examine all calming measures and pick them apart or nurse them, depending on how you see it.

When it comes to the welfare office, I'm not a good advisor, and perhaps if I say nobody should ever go to the welfare office I'm not the neoliberal left-winger from the beginning of this book, but a deeply scared left-winger. I'm excessively afraid of the welfare office and its consequences and papers and questions. I always think of the woman who broke the door as she slammed it in rage when leaving the welfare office, which I think is a great way to leave the place. A person could actually arrive there that way or set out on the bland trip to the welfare office for the sole purpose of destroying its doors. It has to be done; that building, which in my case looks like a prison, like a successful copy of standardized prison architecture, has to be stomped to the ground, beginning, for example, with the doors.

Later, once I've seen the play and would like to watch it all over again and have an apartment inside the play as well as my chestnut tree office so that I never have to leave the play, or only ever briefly, later I don't want to interfere with your thoughts any more. Instead, I'll let you take the trash and the paper recycling down to the backyard, and meet the neighbor Frau Bertram on the stairs on the way back to your apartment. She's just opening her front door.

Are you on your way back from the early shift when we run into each other in the afternoon? you ask her, because the idea comes into your head.

No, Frau Bertram shakes her head, I've usually been shopping. I'm unemployed.

Are you? you say.

Yes, Frau Bertram nods. Unfortunately, she says. She says she used to work as a book binder, specializing in hardcovers, but that was over long ago and now she has to go on one program here, one program there, and in between they give her the runaround.

Do you have to write job applications? you ask her.

Yes, says Frau Bertram, but I don't write as many as I'm supposed to these days, there's no point.

And at the welfare office, you ask, what's it like there?

Don't ask, says Frau Bertram. You just have to put up with it, you have to swallow everything, there's nothing else you can do, otherwise they take away the last of your money.

Frau Bertram starts crying. You notice how porous all fate is and you understand the leap into hoping. Hoping for the deus ex machina, hoping for a superhero or anyone, really—all that's perfectly understandable here in the stairwell with your quietly weeping neighbor Frau Bertram, but five minutes later and three floors higher it's already forgotten. The whole welfare thing, you think, perhaps a person could manage it somehow. It must be possible. A person could regard it as a profession they're performing, something that's not pleasant but at least doesn't require forty hours' attendance a week. So you're considering becoming a welfare recipient and replacing the global corporation with the welfare office. You call out in my direction: I'm going to champion the activity of receiving welfare as a recognized profession. You act the militant but it's nothing but circular motions in your underchallenged head, which has had nothing to do while your body was recovering. As a precaution, you lie down uncovered beneath the open window and shiver with cold, hoping to extend the length of your illness and get more time to think. But your body disappoints you, drives you beneath the covers after only ten minutes, preferring to warm up. You know the way to the welfare office from people's stories, you know you can get there without changing trams.

A day later, I'm back on a train again, thinking about you. I simply wipe the thoughts of welfare out of your head, thoughts that stagger around regular payments. That desire for welfare is now only one of many other lusts, none of which you succumb to. A lust you'll soon have forgotten. A little like a mood. I go too far on my train, miss my stop, and am surprised at myself. I know, everyone could sometimes do with someone to take care of them, and you're alone and you have all the needs a person can have.

You surf the net listlessly and get stuck on an article about frustrated employees at risk of burning out. The article says employees should make suggestions to their bosses about how to improve their work situations. Seeing as every boss can apparently be expected to say no, the workers should ask for a week to try out the suggestion. The boss, allegedly—and you read this three times because you can hardly believe it—will be happy to grant a week's trial, and will assume a week will make the troublemaker see reason, but will then be surprised to see that everything works perfectly well. The boss will subsequently be impressed and accept the suggestion. This article is your little church, in which you let words you want to believe in give you strength.

Well, well, you think, and you really are back to health just in time for the end of your sick leave. You inform your manager of this fact.

Eight

It's easy to make you happy right now. How about this, for example? You walk through the snow that's fallen overnight. You hurry, not for fear of arriving late but so that you're the first to set foot on all your paths this morning. All snow belongs to you. At least for a few minutes, until you're closer to the tram stop where others will use your snow; you'll be happy to share the snow with everyone then. You think of Chekhov's alleged last words, "It's a long time since I drank champagne," and you think: It's a long time since I walked through snow. Although these could be last words, they're actually opening words again, and they tell you, for whatever reason, that something is right because it's snowing, that something is good because it's snowing. The snow falls and falls, stoical or cheerful, depending on how you see it.

You sit on the tram. I see you sitting, see the age settling into your face in the stark tram light; it is still disguised as tiredness. You really do look tired, that's the way faces are in the early morning, all faces around you are tired. People yawn loudly. To your left, though, stands a woman who answers her sitting coworkers' questions about the past night, or doesn't answer them, in fact.

Yes, she says, making no effort to speak quietly. We went to the movie theater and then we left the movie theater. And then we went to my place.

Your place? the other women ask.

Uh-huh, says the woman, and giggles.

You're blushing, her workmates say, and laugh. You didn't get much sleep, then.

He walked me to the tram stop, says the giggly woman.

It won't stay that way, says one woman. Enjoy it while it lasts.

Doesn't he have a job? asks the other woman, and then you start listening more closely.

Not right now, says the woman, and that of course is a clear flaw, that this man who otherwise meets all her requirements doesn't have a job; she'll have to urge him to get one. He's looking for work, she says.

That's what they all say, says one of the others.

No, no, says the giggly woman, he's not like that.

You wipe the window clear with your thick glove. The more the tram fills up with people not wearing office clothes, the clearer a certain anachronism becomes. All this, all the work about to be performed by you and these others like you—and the uncomfortable, crowded commute there and back—fits perfectly into old black-and-white movies, but you're on the way to process a colorful rainbow of contemporary commodities. You, in the midst of your coworkers, in the midst of strangers with coats and bellies, frozen and in some cases chapped hands on hand-holds, are nothing but a placeholder for machines that have already been invented but aren't yet profitable enough to permanently replace you and your workmates, who are very low-cost. The fact that your presence is necessary troubles your employer, who dislikes dealing with troublemakers.

You're a tool gifted with a voice no one wants to hear. Well, they don't have to, you think, and you doze a little more while a longing to make a big entrance builds up inside you, a longing to enter the dispatch hall with panache beyond all measure and to call out loudly: I'm back! Here I am again! And you'd applaud anyone who laughed at your act.

Perhaps the thing that makes you happy is even the specific aspect of the strain, the concentration of all strain upon the body that you're now heading back to. Right now—or not yet, or not any more—you aren't ready to reject this form of effort outright, this effort that challenges only the body and leaves out the mind and its possibilities and especially the possibility of choice. You think you might be able to change something about the work or make something possible, and you think it wouldn't need all that many changes, in theory. You wish you could organize the work in such a way that it wasn't fatal. Yet this wish isn't accompanied by specific ideas, and as soon as you have an idea to put into practice you see an army of head-shakers and brusher-offers before you, around you, and above all inside you, all of them saying: Nonsense, that won't work. This army inside you is what you have to get past. Presumably you weren't and aren't—outside of this book—a person with armies standing at attention inside you, but that's different now.

This work is, and remains for the time being, fatal; that's what I assume. Of course, I can't prove that the work kills anyone. So the question would be justified: Who dies? They're all standing upright and working well and haven't even caught swine flu, because this perfectly organized employer has all the stair rails cleaned at regular intervals.

You doze a little more, carrying the feeling that something might be changed for the better toward your destination, like carrying a cake baked the night before to a party.

In renewed health, you observe with affection the hurrying mass of colleagues sliding or stomping through the snow, and you think: All the things we could do. A woman bumps into you and you're pushed against the tram ready to depart, quickly securing your stance. I think of solidarity, that tenderness between nations that would have to be preceded by tenderness between individuals. You think: We can stop the traffic if we step onto the street as a long, broad group and don't stop walking, and don't care whether the lights are red or green, we'll walk because we'll be a walking we, and we'll simply walk on and on, won't thread through the turnstile and won't go up the stairs in the Banana Tower or over the metal bridge or past anyone who might tell us off.

You want the company to be afraid, you want people to look out of the company's rare windows and see everyone walking past the building. But you don't want to shock the company to its core today, you'd rather educate it and you clearly don't know how impossible education is in the business sector, how impossible it might even be in most other sectors.

You walk through the snow with the snaking line of co-workers, crossing the parking lot. The snake is broken down into segments by the turnstile and then, I'd say, it's all over for the potential, then the potential turns into a wish, aimed at the near or further future: at the end of the shift, at the weekend, annual vacation, retirement. The snake has had its fangs pulled.

What state was that snake in before its fangs were pulled?

What state were the snake's fangs in before they were pulled?

What kind of fangs were they?

What kind of snake was it?

And what exactly was supposed to happen?

Having thought your thoughts before you, I think now: Perhaps there is no more potential, perhaps nothing can be made out of this crowd of people, nothing at all. What if they did all go on walking? Oh, it would be fantastic. But most people in the crowd know, and know from experience: then they'd be out of a job. They'd get no wages and nothing from the welfare office either. And they'd suddenly have time on their hands and wouldn't know what to do. There wouldn't yet be any new ideas suitable for daily life—when would they have been developed? No one has time on their hands here, everyone's tired here. Everyone who went on walking would be replaced in due time, they'd be nothing but the cause of a minor temporary personnel shortage expressed in a single sentence on the company website: Due to poor weather conditions, we currently anticipate delivery delays of up to three days. We apologize for any inconvenience.

So you think: What can all these employees do, and who among my coworkers thinks about what they do with their work, and about what could be done?

And I think: What if the fact that everything that's done serves merely to survive and get through life and in the end benefits only the company, what if that were to turn into the question of the benefit of the benefit? That is, if more than just a few people were to ask, with or without Gotthold Ephraim Lessing: "And what is the benefit of the benefit?"

Until you reach your locker you're accompanied by potentially likeminded people, you're at one with yourself and the mistress of your mind. You consider setting up a writing group and getting your coworkers to write, collecting stories and telling them all: Write down what it's like for you—that matters. Or: Tell me about it, I'll pass on your stories. That would be something, you think. And yes, it would be quite something. That would be the only real benefit of this company.

You're not yet in a hurry today. The snow has calmed your nerves. Or what is it? For the first time, you see photos on the wall outside the changing rooms, and you wonder: Have they always been there? They depict employees celebrating, employees wearing party hats, raising glasses, and blowing kisses at the photographer. All the pictures were taken in the cafeteria, the drink dispensers decorated with paper garlands. When did they ever manage to have what looks like a real party here? you ask yourself. As though it had all happened behind your back. As though you were the only one not invited. You haven't previously entertained the thought that anyone would stay here longer than necessary.

You lean against the coats, sinking briefly into softness. Behind you, a woman is talking about what she had to receive the day before: whips, rubber sheets, asses in boxes, asses in sizes S, M, L, XL. Sounds like fun, someone says. Outside, the snow-covered terrace, the smokers dashing across it for one last cigarette before their shift. Everyone looks as though the snow were chilling them excessively, as though it were punishing them and asking too much of them, something cruel and unusual. You, though, are a declaration of war on hardness and especially on the impression that an employer has you in the palm of its hand here. You spurn that hand clearly grasping at all employees. In German, a language you speak and dream like a native right now, rarely noticing its often very literal nature, the word for employer means literally "labor-giver." And the word for employee means literally "labor-taker." Friedrich Engels heartily disapproved, calling the terms "gibberish." If you like, and perhaps even if you don't, think of the writer Helga Novak:

> The owner of the meat-packing plant takes my work.
>
> He takes it from me.
>
> I, owning nothing, give him my work. HE is the taker of work.
>
> I am the GIVER of work.
>
> Taker and giver of work—at his hunter-green table, we face one another with interchanged names and size each other up.

And yes, you're the one giving your labor, and you'd like to enjoy doing so. As if to your own surprise, you return to work after your illness to begin anew.

You take your box off the shelf, that tiny scrap of home. You look inside; it doesn't look like anyone's rifled through it.

Grit and Stefanie look as though they want to rub their eyes in amazement at the sight of you. We thought you wouldn't be coming back.

I was just sick, you say.

Aha, says Grit.

Grit, whispering more than speaking, has a scarf wrapped around her neck, and Stefanie's wearing a bandage on her right wrist. Everyone seems to be dragging themselves to work and discussing illnesses setting in, on their way out, or in full bloom. As though they got paid for their sicknesses or were taking part in a competition for the worst illness. They're all bearing crosses and afflictions, and only you are like a grasshopper with not a care in the world, landed accidentally on the morning-cool summer sheets of a bedroom, transformed there into a satisfied person until you turn back into a grasshopper and hop along your way.

Incidentally, you learn here, everyone has their own snow. You have your good, humorous snow. Hans-Peter, who turns up again now and receives a joyful greeting from Grit and Stefanie, has goddamn snow. You know that kind of snow well from my parents. It's possible that almost all employees have goddamn snow, because the snow makes it hard for them to get to work and keeps them from arriving on time. People take the snow personally and say: No one cares what trouble we have when it snows. It's all down to us. The snow is nothing but the instrument of a gigantic power.

The morning motivation circle begins. The docks aren't that full today, Mirko says, but what you see and hear is an exhorting choir of invalids who have worked themselves to the bone, a committee telling you: You've recovered. Now work, at long last. We were here and we didn't get a chance to recover!

You don't find your name on any list; perhaps your employer didn't expect you back either. You ask and are sent to Prep, but you don't know where that is. Falk, one of the managers, takes you to Heiner, who runs the Prep department where products are packed in plastic bags. Heiner sees you coming and yells loudly that he asked for help much earlier. Five days ago, he says, and now you're sending me this skinny little chicken. He stretches out an arm to point to a workstation next to him. You have to take fliers for a dance event, bundled in 250-flier piles inside of boxes, put them into bags, and provide the bags with a label legible for machines and humans, describing what's inside each one.

You empty five boxes of fliers and have the next five boxes brought to your workstation.

You're not as weak as you look, Heiner says.

You tell him he's not as much of a bully as he tries to act.

A bully? Heiner asks.

Yes, you say, you're almost scary.

Ach, says Heiner, you don't get far here with *Hello, how you doing, can I help you in any way?* I'm not made of stone.

Well, that's good, then, you say.

Heiner holds up a dog basket that needs packaging. This would be just right for my Trixi.

Who's that? you ask.

Heiner launches into a long story, a monologue he's not performing for the first time, you can tell. He's a guy who needs a stage; the most easily accessible stage is the one you're on right now. Trixi von Trautdorf, Heiner expands, is one of three Tibetan breeds of dog. She was bred in a monastery and she doesn't bark; they trained her out of barking. Trixi is very particular; she won't eat dog food with gravy, she won't go outside in the rain, but she's never had a problem with snow. She's like my daughter. I'm divorced, says Heiner. My daughter does come to visit, but Trixi's my full-time daughter now. Back when I moved out after the divorce, my real daughter decided I should take the family parakeet with me to my new apartment so I wouldn't get lonely. Then Trixi bit the bird's head off, unfortunately. She's a very friendly dog, she was just playing, and no one could have seen it coming because she always let the parakeet perch on her nose and her back, but one day she wiped it out in passing. I bought a new parakeet that looked a lot like the old one, and hoped my daughter wouldn't notice.

And did she notice? you ask.

I don't think so, says Heiner.

You apply labels and listen. It could go on like this; you could spend your time like this until the end of your seasonal job. But then Falk comes over and collects you. Heiner complains, pointing out the boxes full of products still needing packaging. Falk shrugs and says: I'm keeping an eye on it.

Heiner says: I'm keeping an eye on you.

Falk takes you to your next workplace, on a conveyor. You breathe a sigh of relief because there's a gigantic crate full of books there. You rejoice. Why this joy over a pile of books? Why is it so much better to process books and not other products? And is it then also better if the majority of the books are boring and bad or at least look that way?

You say, and you'll stick to your position: It's just better.

Once I was no longer a seasonal associate and had more time on my hands again, I said: Maybe it was good working with books because every book could have been an accusation—you haven't had a book published for a real long time, and now you're here instead. That didn't happen, though. Apart from that book written by the guy I knew, the books didn't torment me and didn't accuse me of anything, they were simply there while I was paid to receive them, and I could get an idea of what people were reading and would be reading. I didn't often think of the bookstores losing customers; I thought more of myself and something that might almost have been called job satisfaction or market research, as far as circumstances allowed.

Beside you, then, more than a cubic meter of books. You take book after book out of the box and everything is just neat now, because every book is its own neatness, and because a box full of books is also neat because it simply can't be a mess—then the books would get damaged.

You receive book after book:

The Royal Treatment.
The Hunt.
Superheroes on Duty.
Light My Fire.
Kiki's Delivery Service.
The Sound of the North.
Decisive Leadership in All Directions.
How Do I Survive Love?
Skeleton Key.
The Submarine of 1000 Dangers.
The Dog, the Crow, the Om … and Me! My Yoga
    Diary.
Marked: House of Night 1.
The Gift.
Sworn to Silence.
The Original Vampire Diaries.

And so on.

You look around. There are only women working around you. When the doors to the gates open, you see men in hats and thick jackets loading and unloading the trucks. Snow is still falling beyond the docks, a few snowflakes riding the draft to where you're standing.

During the break, Stefanie sits down next to you.

Is Grit not here? you ask.

Stefanie says Grit's working in Outbound now and their break is later. I'm in love, she blurts out; she's forgotten to be taciturn with you. It's great, she goes on. You should fall in love, it's great.

Where does he work, or where does she work? you ask.

He works in Stowing, says Stefanie. I was there for a couple days too. We had all this eye contact through the shelves yesterday.

You eat while you listen, and you see Stefanie being light, light the way people newly in love are light.

Purely prophylactically, I whisper in your ear that it's only beneficial for a company if its employees fall in love on its premises, practically fall in love with the company, because then they'll work more blithely and create automatic attachment to the respective company. An infatuation means their labor power is multiplied by the power of love, and is therefore an additional power source for the employees, from which the company profits. Infatuation helps the company get through the holiday season, for instance.

That has no great influence on you. In any case, by the end of the day you'll come to the following sober conclusion: In the same measure as the company is strengthened by infatuated employees, it is weakened by lovesickness, precisely when the formerly infatuated start avoiding each other, when they bicker, brood, grieve, or make jealous observations. The extinguished power of love thus weakens their labor power and consequently offsets the company's initial profit from the employees' infatuation.

I disagree, though: The company isn't harmed, the company measures all time precisely, how much you work when, and makes sure you don't fall below the norm. If you do, you get shunted around within the company to an area where your lovesickness is less of a hindrance, or—your contract being terminable at any time anyway—you just get fired.

The orange vests of the coworkers sitting opposite you are reflected in the windowpane, draped over the field outside the window, depicted there as dull warning lines, occasionally extinguished by the headlights of passing cars. Good luck, you say, interrupting Stefanie in the middle of her considerations as to whether to speak to the man or not. Sure you should, you say. You put your food away, acting like you're in a rush, and you finish up your sandwiches standing in the changing room.

What's up with you now? You seem strangely distracted, almost like you've been caught out. As though something major had occurred to you that now absolutely has to be dealt with. As though you had to work out a way to steal away from your work unnoticed to deal with the matter.

You've got a crush as well. You hadn't noticed it before. Now it's clear, though. When did it start? You couldn't say, exactly. It just kind of developed, and now it's obvious. You feel funny now, a little bit common or garden variety. You wonder whether infatuation is in the air here, whether everyone falls in love with a workmate after a few weeks with the company and, if so, what that might reveal about your feelings. You don't know, and you decide to keep your crush to yourself anyway, and not to consider it anything special for that very reason.

So there's this forklift driver you like; you don't know his name. You're so infatuated you can't look him in the eye. As soon as he approaches you turn away, first taking off your glasses, casting a glance down at yourself, paying attention to your posture, standing straight and acting savvy. It would be no surprise if my old girlfriends from school were to peek out of a box of books to stage-whisper at you: Say something to him, go on! You think he's watching you. You blush when you think he's nearby. You think you see him driving every forklift, this man for whom you suddenly feel something. You're so flustered, you confuse him with all other men. To be precise, it's like the Pavlov thing, the dog and the bell—which, as Heinz von Förster once said in a lecture, rang mainly for the scientist; for the dog, the sight of the bell was enough to get the saliva flowing. Or how much less sufficed for the dog? For you, in any case, the sound of an approaching forklift suffices, the sound makes your heart flutter and the bottom drop out of your stomach, but you wouldn't want to see it like that. Now you even start feeling at home in your emotional turmoil, taking your blushing as a signal that you ought to try and get a permanent contract. You change sides through flights of fancy, exchanging my professions, where a person never knows what anything should cost and when the money will be coming in, for a wish for a permanent contract at this place. Knowing exactly how you feel, of course, I suppose I shouldn't be surprised; but I am. Why all these feelings of yours all of a sudden? You're nothing like this really. And above all, not long ago you had plans for the company and not just for your private working life. So?

No reaction on your end; you're busy receiving books and also with nursing and reining in your emotional state. But I know you, and I know where your feelings come from: you've just watched too much TV. You'd never admit it but you think of this simple solution: You enter the forklift driver's heart, whereupon the forklift driver skillfully maneuvers you into a permanent contract. He carries you over the actual threshold of the company. From there on in, you'll have a life that can be narrated in easily under-standable phrases.

I'm afraid you have a Friday-night made-for-TV-movie heart, which believes a person has to have the kind of love that's in no way threatening or challenging. A nerve-calming kind of love, a bench in the sun with shaded spots as and when required. You wouldn't say that, though. You'd say: Hey, it just happened.

In the meantime I think of my friend Anke, who likes telling me about a job she had at Berlin's international cultural center, the Haus der Kulturen der Welt. She and all the other temporary workers hired to guard an exhibition wore uniforms and were given a guided tour by the curator's assistant, who wasn't in uniform. The assistant told them one of the pieces had been influenced by the work of Paul Bourdieu, whereupon one guy from the circle of prospective museum guides asked whether he was Pierre Bourdieu's little brother, whereupon most of the uniformed prospective museum guards laughed. The curator's assistant didn't understand why they were laughing. The uniformed group went on giggling, and giggled itself into a kind of desperation, or giggled a kind of desperation out of itself, because those who were being told something knew more than the person telling them. Later on, the poorly paid but very well-educated uniformed guards would sit on a staircase in the HKW building for their lunch break where they looked, Anke said, like aged boarding school students who had long since grown out of their uniforms.

You can stay, I say. You can let your brain come to a standstill in this place. But you won't stay anyway. It's simply the case that "life, which for all other animal species is the very essence of their being, becomes a burden to man because of his innate 'repugnance to futility.'" And because you are me, and I am like everyone else in essence, you can't take any additional burden, especially not that burden of futile activity that you—understandably and yet inappropriately—are trying to mask with a crush and a belief in the necessity of a permanent contract.

You press the button to switch on the red light above your workplace, which signals to the forklift drivers that you need a new delivery. The book box next to you is empty and you wait for more books, as nervous as before a first date.

And the forklift driver you're thinking of really does come driving up, but he hasn't got any units on his truck. He says if you haven't got anything to do you should go find Falk at the lead desk. He looks past you, his gaze slightly slanting. You don't reply, just head straight off, instantly forgetting what his voice sounds like. You go over to Falk, feeling glances that the driver isn't sending after you. Falk looks up and then looks straight down again.

Yeah, he says. You get started then.

Doing what? you ask.

Didn't he tell you? asks Falk.

No, you say.

He was supposed to tell you though.

Maybe he forgot.

Yeah, says Falk. Aren't you cold just in a T-shirt?

No, you say. I just had to do a lot of lifting.

Alright, says Falk. He finishes something on the computer. Then he looks up: We value cleanliness, so we use the time when we don't have any inbound shipments to make the hall cleaner. Go and sweep up the Receiving section, please.

Where exactly is that? you ask.

It goes from underneath the conveyor on the one side to the managers' glass box on the other side.

You get yourself a broom, bucket, dustpan, and brush. You start sweeping the floor, brushing up dust that makes you cough, and you don't know where to start. The hall is hard to clean; remains of old strips of tape are stuck to the floor, impossible to sweep up and gathering dirt. You start by sweeping up the most obvious dirt but then you get more precise. Losing your bearings, you sweep some spots twice over. You can't see an end to the task; it feels like you're supposed to sweep a whole residential district. You sweep and sweep but there's a crack in the dustpan and it doesn't pick up the dirt well. You sweep along the side of the glass box, watching the managers you were told at the beginning had an open ear for all your concerns, but you fear any concerns that got poured into the glass box would leak out again through the chinks between the panes.

Inside the glass box, everyone works alone, each at their own computer, absorbed, sitting with bent backs, staring at screens. You sweep the place like a powerful woman, upright and strong, drawing the broom along the edge of the glass box with force; you want them to hear inside that you're sweeping, that someone's sweeping around the managers' box. You sweep around employees' legs too, and they feel sorry for you: Are they already finding work for idle hands? one coworker asks you.

It's OK, you say. At least I'm not just standing around.

You're covered in a thin layer of dust and haven't yet swept a third of the space, when Falk turns up again.

Are you still sweeping? he says. I didn't see you doing it.

I haven't finished yet, you say.

Falk tells you a new delivery's come in so you can go back to your workstation. You watch him walk away and you're surprised it no longer matters whether you've finished sweeping or not. He didn't even ask how far you'd got.

While you head back to your workstation, it occurs to you that perhaps neither the forklift driver nor Falk wanted to tell you to sweep the floor, because sweeping the floor must seem like a punishment seeing as no one else swept the floor, seeing as everyone else stood at their desks and fiddled around with the meager influx of products. They'd both counted on the other, so as not to have to pass on the message themselves.

Aha, I say, and what's that? You try to put on a calm and quiet smile, as though you had an important secret, but you don't quite manage it. Is that supposed to be something, I ask, is that something other than shyness or cowardliness or lack of practice at passing on instructions, or something even more profane?

Ach, you want hearts and flowers, you want to be seen here and looked after and treated nicely, and you wish a clear connection could be made to that Heinrich Böll story where a war invalid works as a people-counter on a bridge and counts all the people, except for his beloved. He doesn't want to include her in any statistic. Not doing so seems to him almost like saving her twice a day from a silent death amidst the numbers. Sure, I say, so what? It's clear as day, you say— even though you and I never talk directly to each other. You want to be looked at in that tender way too and you have no time for tender looks elsewhere. I understand. And you understand too. You've demonstrated to yourself how a person might save herself from dull work that's both too much and too little of a challenge. You'd kind of like it in real life, but you won't get this here in real life. I stuff a stance into your body so you don't shuffle around the hall with no backbone. While you receive a few hundred more books, I drag you out of the last vestiges of infatuation with a fast, rough jerk, like rescuing a child who's fallen in a pond. Not that one hearty grab is enough in your case. I have to pull a couple of times, pluck you out of your feelings and bring you back to your morning state when your infatuation was a sub-text at most, which you'd neither tracked down nor decoded. And yes: you're overdue for a refresher course in feminism. You rub your eyes, tie your ponytail anew, take a seat on an upturned tote. You play hooky for the last few minutes of your shift, and you notice this possibility of not being in love after all laid out before you like one of at least two paths. There, I tell you—you take that path. And although you have a spoiled, sentimental heart, you've almost come back to your senses and you don't actually need this final scene, which comes nonetheless. So you make your way to the line at the time clock and you see the forklift driver. He's wrapped his arms around the waist of a problem solver from behind, his head on her shoulder. That's hardly bothering you now, I say. You look closely and you're not so sure either.

On the tram, there's a free seat next to an older man drinking beer, who looks unkempt but is wearing a neat hat with a crisp brim, not a bit tattered. An empty seat is a rarity at this time of day. You push your way through to it. You've been through a kind of breakup. With effort and willpower, you've returned from a possible future to the present day, and you can barely remember your morning ideas and plans. All you need now is a seat. The man reeks but you sit down anyway and try to breathe through your mouth.

The man raises his beer bottle in salute to you. I'm a professional passenger, he says. I just ride the trams all day long and I come from Herzberg so that means my heart's in the right place, see: *Herz Berg* means heart hill. So I can't work, I have to ride the trams.

You nod and then close your eyes; the man has nothing new to tell you. Your stopover at the bank's statement printer is more important, a trip you make mainly to prove to yourself that you're not doing well, not only with regard to your unmasked and now redundant infatuation. Contrary to your expectations, though, there's new money in your account. That means Amazon has deposited your first paycheck. Your account is still overdrawn, but being accustomed to overdrafts, you hardly register that.

You wander into a trekking store and try out walking shoes. You take a walk along an artificial path made of big rocks, a wooden bridge, and a smooth surface imitating ice. You leave the shoes on, pay for them, and walk back out into the snow. You have purchasing power, albeit limited, and you have walking power. You take firm steps, not slipping, and you have warm feet. In a plastic bag, you carry your old boots with their splintered soles that are no good for winter. You stop at the Christmas market, due to open in a few hours' time, and you find the determination to stuff the old boots in a trashcan. I, whose boots you're throwing away, I did it differently; I wore the boots home, put them on again in spring, and simply couldn't let them go, even though they were really tatty inside and out. I liked the boots too much to throw them away, and I thought: Better to keep hold of things. You never know.

Nine

It's nearly time to come to an end, and I assume you have other plans and don't want to work as a seasonal associate for longer than necessary, so we'll skip a few more days, as we've been doing all along. Actually it's me who's doing the skipping. By now you're doing more of a shuffle, walking sedately with heavy feet, almost always aching. You have only two more weeks to go according to your contract, but you won't end up working those two weeks—though you don't know that yet. The holidays are approaching relentlessly, a horrifying prospect when you think of the turmoil of commodities in the dispatch center. When you think of the end of your contract that coincides with the Christmas holiday, though, it's more of a life raft.

You've spent some of your first paycheck on a traditional German Christmas pyramid from eBay. When it arrives you see that one side of the pyramid is black with burn marks from the candles and there's also a sheep missing, a tiny, finely carved wooden sheep with a pink head. That, at least, you find in the box among scrunched-up newspaper. You set up the pyramid, insert the propellers, fix candles in the holders, and light them. The pyramid refuses to turn. You blow on the propellers and then it kind of works, but not really. You check whether you've put it together right, putting the fallen-off sheep in its place, but the pyramid still won't turn. You take it apart, shove it back in the box, and put the box on the balcony. You feel like kicking it down to the backyard but there are children playing down there.

Christmas, that thing. Christmas, the holiday the whole year seems to build toward. You're going to have to find something else. The Christmas you're thinking of won't show up in your life. And if it did put in an appearance as you imagine it, you'd steer straight past it, repulsed.

The Christmas market has been open for a few days now and doesn't interest you much. Still, you meet a friend there on the way home for a mug of mulled wine. You drink fast and order another to get a bit drunk and a bit warmer. Around you and your girlfriend is a group of young men, who edge closer (each of the men has a mulled wine in one hand and in the other a giant XXL bratwurst, or two mulled wines and two giant XXL bratwursts). You end up in a cluster of men, whose topic of conversation seems to be you and your friend Miriam.

The two of you retreat, escaping the group, and find yourselves standing on a raised pile of snow, as though you could view the whole world. You'd really be better off in a museum, so you drink up hastily, link arms with your friend, and head for the fine arts museum. You can breathe easily now. You immerse yourself in details, you become details in the pictures, cast yourself off, and you've really missed the walking and looking and closer and further and closer again, there's been no time for all that. In your short time as a seasonal associate, you've already racked up quite a deficit, but of course you'll get that sorted out again. Just not right away. It's only a matter of time, a matter of a few days to be precise. So you could actually calm your nerves, but I don't advise calm. I don't advise calm to anyone in this respect. You need neither calm nor patience—cast off all patience, which in any case is only an imitation of real patience. Your patience, channeled into holding out, would be obedience, would be belief in the necessity of having to perform a whole load of work for a tiny scrap of money, would be nothing but an appeasement reflex. Please stay uncalm and notice the deficit, which in your case is actually not yet an exorbitant one. But add it up— what would happen if you stayed with Amazon or a comparable employer, what would be the possible compensation and travel and recuperation?

You're not dead, that much is for sure. You're alive in the physiological sense, and also alive in the figurative sense, but your potential lies deeper than usual, buried beneath your fatigue. You count the days, calling each day *one day down* and heading for a boundary, a dotted line of a fold-in that you'll subsequently place on top of the other dotted line located before the beginning of the seasonal associate job or, even better, before the time when it became necessary to take a seasonal associate job. You'll know that this period of time, which brought you predictable experiences and a little money, is folded away safely between the two dotted lines, you'll separate it from the time before and the time in the future and keep it in a different place—or, even better, you'll lose it.

You're as exhausted as I was; I'd fall asleep spontaneously every afternoon and have children plucking at my eyelids, trying to get back into my view. Play with us! the children said, and I said yes but then fell asleep again, and thought: I'd like to but I don't want to. Leave me in peace. I need to sleep.

The family, incidentally, is the employee's continuous, irritating background noise. The family is what the worker hears when they'd like to recover from work, whatever the work. The worker prefers to see their family asleep, and it's not the employee's heart speaking then, it's their tired body. You'll understand all that when you collapse in the end. To be precise, you'll say: A person can hardly manage to work a forty-hour week, if a person works such a week. It's all too much. And what Byung-Chul Han writes is true: "There's no way to form a revolutionary mass out of exhausted, depressed, isolated individuals."

In the museum, you link arms with Miriam, strolling with no specific destination, at one point heading toward Böcklin's painting *Isle of the Dead* at one end of a long series of interconnecting rooms. As always, the picture is surprisingly small, and as always you're surprised to discover Böcklin's initials on one of the burial chambers. Prepared for the surprise, you move closer to the picture, but then someone stands in front of the painting and doesn't want to look at it at all, instead inspecting something invisible, apparently dangled from his forefinger and thumb. Perhaps, you say quietly to Miriam, he's holding the world. Yes, he really does think he's holding the world in his hand. You step up to him and flick at the supposedly dangling object, but you don't see the man himself very well; his curls form a mist around his head. He steps aside and follows you for a while. You speed up, laughing with Miriam, escaping the world-holding nerd through the room with *Saussure's Heart* in it. You duck through the door, passing the pumping silicon heart and shaking off your pursuer. Life feels manageable in the museum today—but soon things will be back to normal and you won't need emotional protection.

So how is it? Miriam asks, meaning work. Gigantic red tobacco pipes dangle from the museum ceiling. Ach, you say, because you don't actually want to talk about it, and aside from that you can't find the words; the moment you name how things are there, everything will become—though similar—totally different.

They've asked you to switch to another group, where they apparently need good people. You liked hearing that. You no longer see the people you used to work alongside. They work the late shift from then on, and you stay on the early shift in the midst of new workmates. What you hadn't considered when you switched: you now have a new manager, a man you used to watch from above when you stood in the midst of your workmates after the early shift to pass through the turnstile out into the world. From the very beginning, you hated this man for the clarity of the way he embodied the idea of a manager, you hated him instantly with a real passion, with a child's unrelativized intensity, because he looks mean, like a show-off whose showing-off is absolutely obvious, but everyone lets him get away with it because he also possesses rhetorical cunning and an arsenal of subtle, targetable insults; a man everyone wants to get rid of quickly so they push him up the career ladder, which is always the wrong direction, in this case and in similar instances. Yes, you tell Miriam, it's silly to hate someone for wearing brilliant white pressed shirts every day in the midst of T-shirts and sweatshirts, but that's the way it is.

Later, you'll transfer your anger and let go of this two-dimensional stereotype of an enemy manager, but for the time being you're stuck in unconstructive mode and don't even remotely think of the possibility of setting aside your childlike hatred of the boss and moving on to critique the structure that enables a boss like that. You've got your teeth into him, you really have no further aim in life—your sights are set only on the destruction of the moment.

The people who are now your coworkers are a tight team of regulars, apparently athletic and well trained, as though there were no bodies among them too soft and pliable, no pain, no lack of enthusiasm for work, no dawdling elements. The safety vests seem to fit them better too; there's no flapping and slapping here. Your vest, though, still keeps slipping off each shoulder in turn. But here, at the back part of the snaking line where you're now waiting in the midst of the other seasonal associates for the shift to start like every day, on this occasion with a slight mulled-wine hangover, all the vests sit loosely and crookedly or have stains on them. You're almost still asleep and you listen with your eyes closed to two women talking behind you. They're discussing their daily routines: up at 2:00 a.m. to catch the train on time, which is often delayed, if it comes at all and isn't replaced by a bus service after a long wait. Then work off the normal hours, then the dash to the main station, then the dash through the main station concourse, always thinking of the short time available, and the attempt to catch a train that hopefully *is* delayed this time because it can't be caught otherwise.

Sometimes it all goes fine, one of the women says.

Ha, says the other, you can count those times on three fingers.

But sometimes everything's perfect, says the first woman.

The slightest delay, though, means the women have to run, so they usually do run, and they usually run in vain.

Then they wait, suddenly decelerated, but that's an illusion. They stroll around the station, which is more of a mall, looking at stores they know by heart. For a bit of money, one of them says, we could tidy up the displays as we go along. Instead, though, they spend an hour's pay on coffee and bread rolls and don't add up what they end up spending, only add up the hours they spend away from home every day: at least fourteen.

You turn around: Where do you come in from?

From Chemnitz, says one of the women.

What? you ask. Why do you come so far? It makes no sense.

The agency sent us.

But isn't there anything in Chemnitz? you ask.

There is, but the agency's giving Amazon priority at the moment. The staff have been told to get the jobs filled here first and then take care of the other places.

You envisage a circular structure of effort, you imagine maps, relief maps with concentric circles of orange or red denoting effort expended to reach the Amazon workplace on time, see your own morning walk to the tram, a trampled path on the map, an efficient walk that takes no detours, multiplied in the region. You see countless little lines of walking and traveling to your destination. It adds up to a map of everyday soil compaction, a map of employees freezing in the morning as they make their way to work. It seems inappropriately brutal to you that there are colleagues getting up and drilling their way through the winter nights while you're still fast asleep. Of course you've heard tales of people who walk miles every day through terrible weather to get to work and back, but those are stories from a time when it was perfectly normal to be subjugated.

The women say they have no choice.

One of those things people say.

The holiday rush has too many people's time in the palm of its hand, that's what I say.

Further forward in the line is a woman you met yesterday in the changing room. She was clearly new and at the same time just as clearly accustomed to being new. She took off her shoes, looking around for a spot to put them in, and she looked relaxed and professional. It could well have been the relaxed habitus of a well-paid specialist, but it was actually the resignation of an accustomed agency worker, an experienced guest worker. €6.75, she said when you asked how much she earned an hour. And she also said: I haven't got a choice.

And of course you could have contradicted her and said: Yes, you do have a choice. But you stood there tired and shocked next to her, like you're standing there tired now; the reflexes you'd need are numbed, so you nodded and now you nod again and you think: That's one way to see it. Yeah, yeah, the fatigued form of realism, the has-been form of realism that's more like nihilism, but you don't want to hear that. I shouldn't spoil your morning with my opinion, I shouldn't go talking, you think in my direction; I should join the line myself and work as hard as you do every day. That just slips out of your mind, and I do understand: you're the one bearing the everyday burden of perfidious wage labor and it's easy for me to talk, I've got it all behind me. But because I don't know what's ahead of me, and because I'd love to rule out perfidious wage labor entirely for myself and for everyone else as well but I can't, I'm trying to make you think and say what's possible, and I'm also trying to remind you that despair's not worth it and that all agency must be retained, that it's essential to act solely for the sake of an action, so that the action is out in the world and can continue its development. Oh yes, you with your new worker's perspective look directly into the pointless nature of action that aims for vague change; you've come to terms with your current employer like with a stagnant relationship, you're just waiting for it to end. You expect nothing of it.

But what do you know about the outcome of an action just begun, what does anyone who begins to act know about the outcome of an action? That's just how it is, as Hannah Arendt writes: "The reason why we are never able to foretell with certainty the outcome and end of any action is simply that action has no end. The process of a single deed can quite literally endure throughout time until mankind itself has come to an end."

By this point, I don't even mean a particularly clever or subtle action. Nor do I mean you ought to be listing arguments against this form of labor and comparable jobs and carefully convincing others that they absolutely have to rebel against work that leaves the employee no space to be human. All I mean is that you ought to have more guts than me and not try to perform your work as well as possible; you should be trying to perform your work badly.

Or, as Elfriede Jelinek writes: "Anyone alive disrupts."

You ought to prove to your employer that you're alive.

How far does your influence extend at Amazon? You receive inbound units and enter them into the system. You could hide products. Perhaps not forever, but at least for a few days, you could conceal products from others and thus remove them from the commodities cycle. You could damage products and pretend they'd arrived already damaged. You could damage them more subtly so that the damage is only revealed once they arrive at the customer. You could not put preordered goods in the tote for pre-ordered goods, so that the customer receives them late. You could sprinkle dust inside the books (only the bad books and the badly made ones), insert Post-its with insults directed at the product's buyers.

And that would just be the beginning. You could come up with lots of little tricks, do things I haven't thought of. Regrettably, I was intimidated and deeply insulted. But you, you could and so you can disrupt. Of course they'd catch you, because everything gets found out in this company, but up to that point you'd have lived a little more in your workplace and you'd have ordered your obedience to retreat.

We're not leaving this book until you've taken action.

My boyfriend, by the way, got another package from Amazon a few days ago, containing a large roll of paper that arrived totally bent. He examined the roll with amazement, then examined the packaging, which was intact, and said: It must have been bent before they packed it. You can tell, he said.

Yes, I said, you can tell, and I took the package back to the post office the next day.

You're standing in the warehouse, waiting for the shift manager's speech. Uwe, a man you don't know but think you do know, presumably simply due to his safety vest and the company's omnipresent first-name basis, hands around a letter. He'd gone through the turnstile with his phone in his pocket, noticed right away that he still had his phone on him, and so turned straight round and went back through the turnstile; the detectors didn't sound an alarm. Without being asked, he told the security guard he had to take his phone to his locker and would be right back. The guard told him to stay where he was, confiscated his phone temporarily, and sent him to talk to the head of security. The security chief warned him and gave him a copy of the warning to sign:

> Uwe has been cautioned and will make sure in future not to take a phone or similar items into the warehouse.
> *Signature*

The letter's now being passed around, and the actually superfluous question is: Where are we here? In another century? Are we seen as first-graders who have to learn new rules? This company, considered as a mother or a father, is failing outright; you can tell by its employee children—they're showing their worst conceivable side. They act like louts, pushing and shoving and staring past each other. Of course you know exactly where you are. You're in a so-called flat hierarchy, in which all flat hierarchists are gagging for an opponent. Or to put it in the words of the German writer Rainald Goetz: "No, you think to yourself the more pushy someone gets about persuading you, I can't be bothered. And the more often some educational target is repeated, the better it's justified, the greater the desire automatically becomes to do the opposite. Just for fun. To annoy the teachers a little." Except that here, people don't dare annoy their teachers; they make do with their peers, at the same time ignoring all they have in common. They all want a clear and simple target that's easier to hit than a whole corporation.

Now everyone who's read Uwe's caution is against the people from the turnstile; you're against the turnstile guys too. It feels good to be against the turnstile guys because it's clear their position in the hierarchy isn't as flat as yours and your coworkers'; they're slightly above you. In fact, on closer inspection, the flatlands on either side of every orange-vested employee are slopes.

There's no mention of the letter at the morning session; instead there's the usual shift welcoming issued by the man you hate. That show-off or "show-off" or actually just show-off does what's referred to with machines as proactive maintenance, intending to do you and your coworkers a favor before any damage comes about, and announces there'll be mandarins for everyone at lunch break because you're a good team. You'll end up keeping an eye out for the mandarins, against your will, and you'll notice there aren't any mandarins. That almost drives you crazy.

The person working next to you today is Melly, which you know because Melly comes up to you, says hello, and tells you her name. You feel like hugging her right there and then. Until that moment, no one working near you has ever introduced themselves. You did it at first, held out your hand to be shaken in my typically German way, but you soon stopped. Now, though, you think you ought to have kept on doing it. Yeah, that would have been something: saying hello to everyone, in your close vicinity, in your further vicinity, shaking hands with just everyone in the dispatch hall and not stopping until everyone had been said hello to, which would have meant devoting your entire workday to saying hello.

You receive books, less interested in the books today than in your new workmate. Melly looks like a movable sculpture and seems like her own muse. You wish you could snuggle up to her; she has breasts and a belly and an ass and soft but strong arms and a friendly face.

You receive a pallet of books. The forklift driver who just brought you the products parks next to you, waiting to pick the received goods up again.

What? you say.

What? he says.

I'm working, you say.

Doesn't look like it, he says.

I'd like to be undisturbed, you say.

I'd like to get on with my job, he says.

You bend down and start removing the plastic from the pallet. On it is Ken Follett, nothing but Ken Follett. The forklift driver climbs down from his vehicle, gives an annoyed sigh, counts the number of books by width, counts them by length, counts the number of layers just as routinely but perhaps wrongly, you suspect, then scans one book, enters the total number, throws the scanner down on the desk, reloads the goods, and drives off. Sweet dreams, he calls out.

It'd been like that for days, since you joined the new shift.

The forklift drivers stick like glue to the workstations here, all the forklift drivers have a saying here, the regular staff come by and fake-joke: Don't mess up our average. The proverbial cold wind blows here. It's pretty much the way you imagined it would be in this global corporation, here. Apart from that, the air smells of aftershave. The scent is refreshed every time a forklift approaches.

The next forklift brings you calendars:

Alpine Panorama Infinity Calendar.
Horses.
Girls and Horses.
Bathroom Romantic.
Watercolor Dreamland.

All oversized and hard to count, but some forklift driver comes along, plucks your sorted piles apart, and says: It's really easy.

Which isn't true. Really, it's not easy, it's not that easy for you, you're having trouble even lifting the calendars and turning them over without damaging them to find their product number.

Melly, the redemptive muse, comes up to you and lets you in on the secret: Everything's different here than on the other shift. They want to be the best here. That's why they're so pushy. And those guys—she points out the nearby workstations occupied mainly by regular team members—they make sure they only get good stuff delivered so they can do their receiving faster. Not hundreds of different books, no fiddly toys, nothing you have to touch. All they get is palletized products. The forklift drivers pick out the good stuff in the docks so that this here stays the best shift. Pallets full of one kind of book, so they can receive five hundred books in five minutes, and they do that all day long. It's the turbo shift, Melly says. You have to get on the forklift guys' good list, then they'll bring you the good stuff.

Are you on their good list? you ask her.

No way, says Melly, I don't care about them. And I don't care about the average either. I'm going back to the other shift next week, I'm not interested in these people here.

You look around and now you understand the leftovers you otherwise had to deal with: difficult cases that needed a solution, products with the wrong numbers not recognized by the system, items that had to be transported all the way across the hall to another section, products that simply needed more done to them than to be received into a tote or onto a pallet. There's no time for those cases on the turbo shift, the turbo shift only deals with the good, fast products. The next shift tackles the leftovers.

There's a cold draft from your right; the dock door won't close properly, again. But on your left is Melly, luminous with her soft brown arms. You do nothing at all for a moment. Suddenly, Sebastian pops up next to you, his feedback sheet thrown down on the desk next to your resting hands. Good morning, he says.

You jolt back to attention. Feedback again? you ask.

We do feedback every day on our shift, Sebastian says. He looks oddly bland, the kind of face that's hard to remember, which looks unfamiliar to you again today. You only recognize him by the hole in his right earlobe. He's got one of those stretched, oversized ear piercings. A hole a centimeter across, held in place by a wooden eyelet. The opening reveals a mole behind it. You look at that mole while Sebastian reels off his statistics: Up to shift level in *small* segment, drastically below level in *medium*, below shift level in *large* as well. It all has to get better. You're not new here any more, honey.

You say: I was good on the other shift.

He says: The other shift doesn't matter. He picks up his sheets and walks on.

You say: But I didn't have any *medium* products.

You were still below the shift average, says Sebastian, putting his feedback sheets down on Melly's desk.

She nods but doesn't listen to him. Sebastian talks in more detail to Melly than to you but she goes on working; he's soliloquizing. Melly the muse doesn't do him the honor of listening; she tells him he's in her way, she can't reach the products, which is bad for her balance as he no doubt knows.

Sebastian moves on. Melly taps a finger against her head. That told him, you say.

No one needs to tell me how to work, I know how to get my work done, Melly says.

They're all crazy here.

I don't care though.

I'm not going to work myself into my grave.

Don't listen to him, he's crazy.

From that point on, the two of you are a coven of witches, and as such a logical reaction to the figures and graphs and the daily admonishments to *work faster, you're under the shift average again*. Every witch is the result of a ridiculous power, not a real witch but a quote, a reference to every fairytale perhaps once told to someone like Sebastian, which secretly still has the strength to shock him. Yes, you want to shock him. You think extravagantly about the prospect and miss the beginning of your lunch break. You look around: Melly's gone. You'd have liked to spend the break with her.

You rush up the stairs, looking out for Melly but not finding her. At least you find Martin in the cafeteria, a guy you worked next to a few days ago. You don't want to shovel your lunch into your mouth alone any more. Martin is sitting with a gray-haired man with a ponytail, Wolfgang, and an older woman, Roswitha, who likes to be called Rosie. Rosie's eating sandwiches from home,

Wolfgang too. Martin is having French fries with curry-wurst, and you have the same pasta as always. White Christmas, says Rosie, we haven't had a white Christmas for ages, and now one's coming when we're locked up in here.

Oh, you say, but there's still time until Christmas.

Wolfgang bites into his sandwich and talks with his mouth full: I'm not that into Christmas, me and my friends go to this cave and burn a tree, that's enough for me, and then Christmas is over. He unpacks another round of sandwiches and inspects their contents. What have I given myself here? he says. I don't like the look of these. He puts the sandwiches away again. I'll have to tell myself off tonight for not eating up.

Fun people, all of them with subtext, and all of them would rather be somewhere else. You wish your lunch break were longer.

In the women's changing room, where you lock up your thermos flask just before the end of the break, Robert, the trainer from the beginning of your time here, is standing in your way. He's distributing empty lockers to new employees. I've seen it all before, he says toward two women changing clothes next to him. One of the new women looks up from taking off her pants and asks where to put her belongings—the empty lockers have no locks on them. Robert puts his hand on her shoulder as she's pulling one leg of her pants over her left foot, and says: A little tip for you, sweetie, buy yourself a padlock.

Good grief, you think, surely it's not that difficult to say something normal. You tell the women what you found out a few days ago: Sometimes the security guards have padlocks you can borrow for a day.

You go back to your workplace. A stocky woman in a luminous green vest is rummaging in the paper-recycling box. You read the words *Security North* on her back. Melly whispers in your ear: It's the sniffer dog. She's checking we haven't hidden anything in the trash to try and smuggle it out of the building.

The sniffer-dog woman's arms are too short to reach the bottom of the recycling box. She just rummages at the surface, shifts folded cardboard boxes from one side to the other, unfolds a measuring stick and stabs it at the bottom. She doesn't look at the employees whose trash she's searching, says nothing on either coming or going. She works as a small gesture of distrust, as a warning message from the higher levels of the flat hierarchy. She limps away; you watch her leaving.

You can't stand any of this today.

You receive the following book: *How to Kill a Frustrating Job: Why It Doesn't Matter Who You Work For*. You read the blurb on the back: "I don't earn enough money. My boss doesn't value my work. Everyone tells me what to do. Every day's the same. All my colleagues are mentally ill. Know the feeling? Congratulations, you've found your dream job! Yes, you read right: the job you have is the best job you can get. Volker Kitz and Manuel Tusch prove convincingly: all jobs are the same in principle, and your frustration at work is down to you. The two job coaches reveal the most frequent reasons for frustration on the job and present a surprisingly effective method for changing and improving your annoying work life of your own accord—guaranteed free of 'Think positive' formulas!"

You take the book over to Melly and read aloud what you've just read. You say: Congratulations, we've found our dream job. You say: Our frustration on the job is down to us.

Oh yeah, Melly says.

Sebastian pops up surprisingly again. You don't know how he manages to sneak up like that.

If you have any questions, please come to me or the more experienced team members. Any questions?

No, says Melly, just answers.

You obviously need another briefing, Sebastian says to you. You have to work faster. You go back to your workplace, rolling your eyes so that Melly can see. You could have come up with something better, of course. Do we have a problem? Sebastian asks.

Yes, you say.

I think so too, says Sebastian.

You stare at the yellowish-brown mole behind his ear.

You need to listen better, he says.

Uh-huh, you say.

Don't talk to me like that, he says.

How do you want me to talk to you? you say, laughing in his face. You're ready to meet him out by the docks for a fist fight. How would it end? You'd be wiped out from punching and taking punches, but something inside you would be satisfied.

Or, actually, you don't ask how he wants you to talk to him and you don't laugh in his face; you say nothing.

He takes a book out of the crate, holds it in front of the scanner, presses Enter, then puts the book in the tote. He repeats this three times. What do you notice? he asks.

You've received three books, you say.

He gives you a provocative stare. I received units without putting them down in between, looking at them and turning them over. I did the quality check and the receiving in a single motion.

Whoop-de-do. But you don't say that either.

Do it again, please, you say. Sebastian repeats the process.

He walks away, calling out as he leaves: And you do it the same way now, if you please.

It's like this: You work as fast as you can, you work at different speeds, and in between you stare at the ceiling without meaning to. If you can do something, that doesn't mean for you that you have to get faster at it. Being able to do something merely calms your nerves because then you have to devote less attention to the work, you can drift off when you feel like it. You're not inherently interested in optimization. You're not inherently against optimization, either; you just don't usually think of optimizing actions. I've never taken a course in speed-reading or speed-typing. Still, you attempt to make more effort, you stop examining the books, you're only interested in speed; it's a kind of downhill race. You make yourself thin, reject all temptation to open up one of the books. But after half an hour you lose focus and then you do open up another book, reading a few lines and relaxing.

The most intensive work here is done by your arm muscles. You've developed really fantastic arm muscles. Soft and strong at the same time. They're a real added value of this work. Or they're secretly the real content. The encounter value arising from the work's contact with your body is your arm muscles, but there's no more encounter value than that.

Next to you is a crate full of similar-looking books, all written by the same woman, hardly any doubles. You receive them in the new single motion, almost elegantly, and you read the titles out loud to Melly:

The Marketing Secret For Dentists: How to Increase Your Turnover in 12 Simple Steps—Without an MBA or a Marketing Budget.

The Marketing Secret For Catering Companies: How to Increase Your Turnover in 12 Simple Steps—Without an MBA or a Marketing Budget.

The Marketing Secret For Fitness Studios: How to Increase Your Turnover in 12 Simple Steps—Without an MBA or a Marketing Budget.

The Marketing Secret For Real-Estate Agents: How to Increase Your Turnover in 12 Simple Steps—Without an MBA or a Marketing Budget.

The Marketing Secret For Hairdressers: How to Increase Your Turnover in 12 Simple Steps—Without an MBA or a Marketing Budget.

The Marketing Secret For Bakers: How to Increase Your Turnover in 12 Simple Steps—Without an MBA or a Marketing Budget.

The Marketing Secret For Alternative Practitioners: How to Increase Your Turnover in 12 Simple Steps—Without an MBA or a Marketing Budget.

The Marketing Secret For IT Consultants: How to Increase Your Turnover in 12 Simple Steps—Without an MBA or a Marketing Budget.

The Marketing Secret For Travel Agencies: How to Increase Your Turnover in 12 Simple Steps—Without an MBA or a Marketing Budget.

The Marketing Secret For Roof Tilers: How to Increase Your Turnover in 12 Simple Steps—Without an MBA or a Marketing Budget.

The Marketing Secret For Facility Cleaners: How to Increase Your Turnover in 12 Simple Steps—Without an MBA or a Marketing Budget.

The Marketing Secret For Metal Workers: How to Increase Your Turnover in 12 Simple Steps—Without an MBA or a Marketing Budget.

The Marketing Secret For Cafés: How to Increase Your Turnover in 12 Simple Steps—Without an MBA or a Marketing Budget.

The Marketing Secret For Kitchen Studios: How to Increase Your Turnover in 12 Simple Steps—Without an MBA or a Marketing Budget.

Etc.

You dissect the word *doable*, the idea these books present that anything is doable, break it down to its individual letters and drag each letter out, revolted. How everything's doable, how everything can be made doable, it's so boring how doable everything is, how even nondoability is doable.

You ask yourself: Is there anything a person has to know to be successful? You know nothing about it.

Your employer, though, knows this: To be successful as a company, it has to at least know the employees' sore spots, because how else is it to stop them from getting boisterous?

That employer knows its employees like to go home on time and inherently believe a shift doesn't realistically end until they've changed their clothes and left the premises. Which is why the workers assume they'll have to go on working at least fifteen unpaid minutes before and after every shift, and therefore start cleaning up their workplaces a little earlier every day. Only seconds, which then become one, two, three minutes that they then line up earlier for the time clock to get to the turnstile quickly, to not be the last link in the tired, snaking line.

The line starts forming in front of the time clock at 2:25 p.m. today, two minutes before the tolerated time, five minutes before the actually allowed time. The problem solvers and team leaders are at the very front of the line. When you join the end of the already considerably long line at 2:27, it rearranges itself. The problem solvers and all the experienced employees have vanished, as if swallowed up by the earth. Right at the front are now new people you've never seen before. It makes for an unfamiliar sight—the new people in the best places. Next to the new staff is a man with a portable desk, a computer on top of it. He looks fresh and clean, doesn't seem to have spent a whole shift in the dust yet. The bearded man with horn-rimmed glasses, presumably Amazon's only hipster, gestures the employees over from the time clock one at a time, checks their employee ID cards, scans their barcodes, and enters their names in a list.

What's he doing? you ask the guy in front of you.

He's writing down the names of the people waiting at the time clock too early.

And why don't they disappear inconspicuously, you wonder.

The hipster doesn't look up, just goes about his work stoically. He doesn't say a word, or are you wrong about that? When the bell rings for the end of the shift, he scans the last ID. Now the experienced employees flood back, line up, and rush outside. The hipster closes his laptop, straightens up, and heads off with his wheeled desk as though he'd never been there.

You think about this performance, asking yourself what it was—a silent drama in which everyone played along, something no one seems to complain about, something that almost might not have been. You climb the steps of the metal staircase, spotting Sebastian ahead of you; he's pushed ahead unnoticed. Between his legs, the frayed ends of his jeans. You turn them into the tentacles of a toxic species of land jellyfish that has settled parasitically in Sebastian and is devouring him from inside without him noticing.

By the way, I met the Amazon hipster once after the end of my seasonal associate job. One morning as I was taking my kids to school, he got out of a car and sorted through bags in the trunk. I didn't know right away where I'd seen him before, but I remembered after I'd watched him for a while. Unable to think of anything better or because it seemed like the most appropriate idea, I called out the name of a book I'd just read, by Mark Greif and others. I yelled at him: *What Was the Hipster*! I called it twice and I thought then he might know he was over.

Ten

It's nearly over; you've nearly made it through. There'll be no need to congratulate you and you won't expect congratulations when the time comes; you'll leave the dispatch hall forever downright casually, you won't stage an impressive closing scene, but if you want you can imagine one afterward, a dramatic exit from the dispatch hall, which I didn't manage when I worked there, not a chance.

But right now it's still early morning, just after five thirty. You can see the tram stop and you hear the tram approaching. You break into a run; the tram is three minutes early. You overlook a curbstone, stumble, slip, fall over. You get up, pause for a moment, scrape the snow out from under the cuffs of your anorak, pat it off your pants. You limp to the stop. The tram's gone. The display illuminates the following message: Dear passengers, due to poor weather conditions, no services are operating.

You look around. The weather's no worse than on other days. Later, you'll learn that it rained during the night and that rain iced up the overhead tram wires because of the cold. Everyone who relies on the trams at this time of day will say: There just weren't any trams running. You'll wonder what tram it could have been that you saw, that you ran after, that no one but you seemed to have seen. For the time being, you read the passenger information over and over. You don't believe no more trams will be coming. You sit down in the shelter and wait.

A Unimog parks across the street and three people in orange work clothes get out of it. Two stand on the sidewalk, the third climbs onto the loading bed. He shovels grit down onto the sidewalk. They look unpracticed, not yet coordinated. While the first guy gets into the front of the truck and lights a cigarette with the window open, his smoking hand stuck out of the window but all the smoke blowing back into the driver's cab, the other two—a man and a woman—pick up buckets, grab small shovels from the loading bed, and start scattering the grit on the path. They don't do it with casual panache. They throw little piles or leave large gaps between the gritted areas, leaning forward to scatter the grit instead of walking calmly and upright with broad strides. This deicing service is elongating time or elongating the activity itself. If the three of them had moved with just a little more practice, a person might have assumed they were experts at killing a long workday, who'd developed a deft choreo-graphy that kept them in motion and displayed activity and absolved them of the suspicion, at least from passersby, that they weren't very keen workers.

You bury your head beneath your hood as best you can and ask yourself what is actually reasonable if you want to turn up at work on time. The wind whooshes into the shelter and you withdraw further into your anorak; you ought to move but you don't want to. No one else is at the tram stop. You feel your employer's breath blowing coldly around your neck beneath your scarf, murmuring: How dare you just sit around and not set out and think of a way to get to work on time? The snow is marvelous but perhaps not quite suitable at this time of day. You think: I can't take the slightest thing, and you wonder how it can be that your employer, your invisible employer, is messing about inside your head.

You've become a person who's permanently cold. You think you've never been as cold as you are every morning and every afternoon now, and sometimes at work as well. That cold is horrible and boring and annoying and by no means comparable to the cold I knew well when I was thirteen. I went to school with my coat undone on even the coldest of days and showed off my bare belly, a bit of it at least, because that was the fashion. I stood in a circle with other girls on a corner near the school, central enough to see, and be seen, by all the teachers and students scurrying to school from all directions. We all rolled up the sleeves of our coats, as though the ends of our sleeves had been sucked inward by a vacuum cleaner. My friend Kerstin's teeth chattered, or Kerstin gnashed her teeth so that it sounded like they were chattering. But no one thought to tell her to dress up warmer. Instead, we all wanted our teeth to chatter like that, all wanted to be so convincingly cold that our teeth chattered, though few of us managed it. While I was terribly cold in the midst of the others, I wasn't a bit cold at the same time. For you, though, the current cold is hurtful.

Incidentally, you've now started talking about the weather. Now that you leave the house and enter it again at fixed times, the weather has become essential. Had you, like me, been reading Thomas Glavinic's book *Das bin doch ich* after a day of seasonal associating, you'd have closed it just like I did. Glavinic didn't understand such interest in the weather and the course it might take, didn't understand it a bit, in fact he found it amusing. Like me, you'd have instantly taken his disinterest personally—his explicit, flaunted lack of interest—and thrown the book on the floor by the bed, an uncharacteristic action. You too would have thought Glavinic simply had too much time on his hands; he filled page after page with reports on his imagined illnesses. I had no time for hypochondria, and you have no time for hypochondria and certainly no interest in it.

The display board at the tram stop has nothing new to report, stubbornly informing passengers that no more trams will be running. You try to join the dots of the city, mentally searching for a good walking route to Amazon. Fed up with sitting, you finally set off. The snow is deep and heavy; it's started snowing again. Ahead of you, a woman struggles with a wheeled suitcase. The case refuses to be pulled along, sometimes glides properly over the snow but then gathers clumps of ice and grit between its wheels and gets stuck or tips over. The woman drags the case upright and then carries it more than she pulls it. You walk past the Fürstenhof Hotel; it looks inviting, protected inside by a layer of sleep and warmth.

At the main station you come across waiting work-mates, a soup of colleagues in a pan full of slushy snow and soaked cigarette butts; in amongst them a newspaper vendor is relentlessly refusing to feel cold, not walking up and down to keep warm and even showing bare skin between his scarf and coat.

You wait, you all wait. Somewhere inside you is a warm spot and you try to reach it, even your feet freezing in your new shoes by now. You walk to and fro, blow on your hands. You blow warm breath into your fur-lined gloves, your middle fingers frozen white.

When the replacement bus arrives you squeeze onto it with the others and now enjoy standing in the jumble of colleagues, not needing to hold on to anything. Let them all come even closer. You'd be happy to drive forever in this slowly warming-up bus. But then everyone gets out, dashes off, rushes across the road at a red light. Everyone pushes into the changing cubicles but no one runs; there's order in the rush. You arrive only five minutes late and you learn: even if you're only five minutes late, you still get a quarter of an hour docked.

You didn't know that.

You join the morning session and hear that everyone has to work over the coming weekend. You rummage in your box for the shift schedule. It says something different. You've got next weekend off. You shrug—it'll get sorted out, you think.

You decide not to work the time you're not getting paid for, and you walk slowly, deliberately slowly, to the furthest restroom. You stay there, sitting on the toilet lid, mindlessly or with your mind racing. Will someone come looking for you? You don't know. You warm your still ice-cold hands under the dryer, which blows hot and loud.

Later you stroll back; you've done all your rushing for today.

The gate between the docks and the hall is stuck again, so a cold wind whooshes across your workstation from the right. You put on a jacket. It barely makes a difference. You go to Sebastian and say you really urgently need a different workstation today. He answers: If you like a nice breeze in the summer you can't complain when it gets too cold in the winter. You don't point out that you haven't yet benefitted from the nice summer breeze and won't benefit from it, either, because you'll be long gone by next summer. Instead, you ask him about the next weekend. Your voice suddenly wavering, you say you don't have to work on the weekend, according to the schedule. You say: I have a day off on Saturday.

Sebastian says that can't be the case because there aren't any weekends off during the preholiday period.

You clear your throat and cough: But that's what it says on my shift plan.

Sebastian says: You can take a break in the new year.

Why in the new year? you ask.

There's no time off before then, he replies.

But my contract ends on December 24th.

Yeah, says Sebastian, they always write that but it's not true, it'd be dumb to let people go on the 24th. We have the most work between Christmas and New Year's, that's when everything gets sent back.

There's presumably no point in speaking to the guy.

You—with your hoarse voice and the question of who has control of you here and what schedules and contracts mean—you open your mouth and then close it again. You're not even a tool with a voice any more.

On top of that, you find not a box of books at your workstation but a pallet of heavy table lamps—and you view this as a punishment. You walk around the lamps, longing for the books.

It's easy, says the forklift guy who doesn't have anything to do right now. Four lamps per crate, four crates per pallet. Are you new here?

You know the score. You find these comments super-fluous, so superfluous they make you want to puke. You go on receiving under the forklift guy's observing gaze, dragging heavy lamps in boxes out of larger boxes onto the desk, then placing them onto a new pallet. Why make it simple when you can make it complicated? says the forklift guy. Right, you say, why does it always have to be simple?

He gives a scornful laugh and drives up closer to you and the pallet. Now you have to watch out you don't trip over the forks.

He drives off.

And where's Melly? You can't spot her anywhere. She's dissolved into air like a night's dream. You receive slowly. You check every box for damage, more carefully than in the previous days, then you take a break and go to the restroom again. Where else could you go? The skylights in the hall have a cover of snow; it feels like being inside a gigantic igloo.

When you get back you arrive at your workstation at the same time as the despised shift manager. He informs you that the head of Europe will be coming in today and the shift wants to show him its best face, so you have to tidy up thoroughly, really thoroughly. So you tidy up, doing that slowly too, before you go on receiving the lamps and then wrapping them in plastic to be transported to the warehouse. The plastic wrap tears over and over, you start over and over from the beginning; perhaps you never want to work fast again.

That's how you make it through to your lunch break. You dawdle through your lunch too, not eating as greedily as usual, and afterward you put your head on your arms and close your eyes.

Clench your teeth, you say to yourself on your way back into the hall. Find synonyms for teeth-clenching, you say to yourself. At least there's now another big box of books next to your workstation, and you open it carefully with your cutter. The box is full of children's coloring books and workbooks. You're disappointed. So you receive workbooks, which the computer informs you have to be packaged first. You miscount frequently and put various books under one product number. But you still send off the offending tote, and others after it. You wonder whether your errors will be noticed and flagged or whether they'll be passed on to customers, since no one here likes dealing with errors, and the customer will be sent a copy of *Filly Fairy: Coloring and Puzzle Fun* instead of *Discoveries 1: Fit for Tests and Quizzes; Workbook with Solutions and CD-ROM, Part 1.*

Shift Manager Christian shows the head of Europe around. He gestures from the aisle at the employee desks. You don't understand what they're saying, just the gestures. Like he's showing off his farm, his field, his herd of cattle. You and your coworkers aren't working for the customers at this moment; you're laboring only to make a good impression. You're like wax models in a mining museum—but of course that's not true, most of your workmates are working normally, it's only you who feels like a wax dummy and is acting contemptuous and audacious. You don't want to be the kind of employee who can be pointed at. You duck down and hide behind the paper-recycling box. You want your workstation to look unoccupied. After squatting down for a while, you get up and look around. You do nothing more than that.

In between the workbooks, a proper book shines through. You shove the workbooks aside and unearth more proper books. At last. Your attention is caught by a book with a bald man on the cover: *Naughty* by Marc Chester, a hooligan telling his story. "The shocking inside story of one of the most organized and violent soccer hooligan gangs currently active in Britain, the Naughty Forty. Written by one of the gang's central figures, it reveals the network of alliances and friendships between leading hooligans across Britain, and the explicit reasons they are so feared."

You don't receive the book; instead, you prop it up on the desk like a family portrait. It feels like you now have a thug with a provocative glare on your side. Marc Chester is your own private thug, he's a friend and you watch him, still shy. You stand in front of the book and say: Marc, those people over there, they're bothering me. You know I wouldn't ask you if it wasn't important to me. But those people over there, they're really bothering me right now and I don't think they'll stop bothering me. Marc Chester's answer: "And the first thing I would like to say is: We're Stoke City, we're Naughty Forty, and we're game as fuck. So let's have it."

Of course the book you need at any moment always exists, and sometimes you're lucky enough to find it when you need it. Marc Chester makes you laugh in any case, and you have him by your side, life-sized. There's one thing you can do because you're me, don't forget: you can think up anything and anyone and imagine them by your side. What you and I can't do, though, because you and I don't want to, is to think your employer into a better employer and to compare these working conditions to even worse, less favorable conditions, so as to say: It's not all that bad. Other places are worse. It used to be worse.

We don't do that. You and I want the best and we're not asking too much.

You pull a book out of the jumble in the box, a book that surprises you like a hidden treasure. A book I have at home, which I like very much, which I've put in your box. It wasn't really in any box of books at Amazon and it's really out of print anyway, but it can be downloaded from the publisher's website: *Loose Associations* by Ryan Gander. I have lots of favorite bits but I'll let you find one that seems particularly appropriate right now. You've zipped your fleece jacket all the way up and you read:

There's a university in Buffalo, in New York State. The campus there was relocated twenty years ago, so the architect could completely redesign it. He built the entire site but didn't put any paths in ... he just left it as gravel. There's very heavy snowfall in New York State in winter, and as the campus began to be used students began to navigate around the campus, leaving paths in the snow, so if there were a lot of people walking on the path, it would end up very wide, and the ones that weren't used so much were narrower. The architect then sent a helicopter up to make an aerial photograph of the campus, then plotted all these desire lines on a map and built the paths in the same positions with the same widths as the desire lines. It's an example of perfect planning of public space.

Desire line, you think, a trodden path, a path most wished-for. A path that comes about when people want to get from one place to another and there isn't yet a path.

And then the time comes, and it's not as if you'd been waiting for it all along. But now that the time's come it *is* as if you'd been waiting for it all along. From now on, at any rate, everything takes place with astounding consistency.

So you suddenly have this thought: I could just stop. I don't have to see it through.

You try it out in a conversation with yourself. But no matter how many conversation partners you think yourself into, they all share your opinion sooner or later, and that is this: I could just stop now. It's enough now.

It's no use reminding yourself of your contract that only lasts until Christmas Eve, or that you were thinking of trying to get a permanent contract only a few days ago. You look out at the street through the open gate. Some workers in the dock are carrying clipboards and checking inbound shipments, others are driving pallets around, sometimes moving them only a few meters until a forklift driver comes to pick them up or to put other goods down next to them. They all know their way around the job.

Now your hands disintegrate and your bones crumble and the wind blows through them. The wind carves a channel of cold into you. As you lift a tote you flinch, flashes running down your arms and up the back of your neck. It takes you three attempts to get the tote onto the conveyor. Your wrists go on stabbing with pain, your back won't bend any more, your knees refuse to either bend or straighten.

So the time really has come, for you.

When you see Sebastian shuffling toward you with the white feedback sheets in his hand, you put down the book you're about to receive and leave your workplace to go to the restroom again. You examine everything in detail: the pallets full of totes in various colors, the damaged pallets, the products waiting to be measured in the totes. The employees at the workstations, laboring industriously or not. You stick accurately to the floor markings and follow the rules for moving through the hall in every detail, not out of defiance or sardonic enjoyment in emphasizing their ridiculousness, but out of fatigue.

This system here is not yours, and you don't understand anything any more because you've understood enough, and nothing here is still worth experiencing.

You think of this woman you saw at the zoo, a while ago now. The woman was telling her son off, asking over and over why he kept yelling, told him to stop yelling, she'd never take him to the zoo again, etc. The boy had long since stopped yelling, though; he'd been calmly walking along next to the woman all along, as if uncoupled—he clearly had plenty of experience of blanking out her litanies. He turned his head away toward the calls of the croaking cockatoos.

You fix your gaze on that boy as you climb the stairs to the restroom. You open the door to the bathroom stall and instantly fall out of the company's time into your own time.

You're now free from all instructions. Sheer perseverance wouldn't make you any better at anything here; it would be nothing but perseverance for perseverance's sake, something that must have been successfully and sustainably extolled at some point by someone who'd profited from the first perseverance of a laboriously persevering person. And what would be gained now from such perseverance, exploited for centuries? Perseverance brings nothing but sweat and money that reeks of rotten arguments. Perseverance tries not to perish and it praises itself for all eternity.

During your remaining working hours, you simply continue to collapse. You let it happen without the slightest inhibition, amazed at this crumbling, this dissolving, and not preventing it in any way. You work slowly, ponderously. You don't count the products in the tote and you refrain from all conscientiousness, entering any old number in the system, which responds by beeping its error alarm. You send the tote off anyway. You carry on like in the morning, except more calmly now. You can no longer be harmed.

You sort through your employee box. You check carefully that no personal objects remain in it. You stuff your notes, Band-Aids, and hairbands in your pockets and close the lid. It can all stay that way until the end of your shift.

Later you empty your locker too. Only the safety vest and the transparent water bottle remain inside. You put your work shoes on the shelf; they'll presumably be thrown away soon. You remove the padlock, move out immediately and entirely, don't hand in your notice but simply leave, placing no importance on being cautious, not pretending that your absence, which will begin the next day, wasn't planned.

The entrance hall is unusually noisy. A cassette recorder is playing "Jingle Bells." Four Santas are swaying to the music, two on either side of a narrow pathway. You squint your eyes to make out the faces behind the masks; the Santas laugh. They look like they're celebrating their own existence. They hand all those leaving a beer mug with the Amazon logo, from the right, and a bag of cookies and chocolate, from the left. You turn them both down at first but then you do reach for the cookies, and eat them as you leave.

And then a choir proclaims:

> What are you doing?
> You can't just stop!
> You coward!
> You lazy thing!
> Work takes skill!
> Work takes some learning!
> Now you know what it's really like!
> And you just cut and run.

But before you listen to the choir, there's one thing you need to know: the choir's just on tape.

Eleven

Well done.

Very good.

You've been through a lot.

I'm very much in favor of leaving the way you left, which is not just due to the fact that I left Amazon the same way you left it and had ended other jobs that way too, for instance skipping out of a call center by the back door or not actually skipping out, but leaving unannounced and unnoticed forever.

With your fixed-term contract, you go back to the doctor the day after your departure, this time with more routine. The doctor wants to sign you off for a week. You say: Please make it until Christmas, that would be better. The doctor writes her sick note according to your requirements. You send the note to Amazon and no longer regard yourself as a seasonal associate.

And apart from that?

You tidy up, you move slowly, you spread yourself out in the day. You can hardly believe your time at Amazon is over.

Another day passes more or less like that.

On the third day, you run into your neighbor Frau Bertram. Frau Bertram points at the newly restored building across the street. The first-floor apartments are so transparent that you can see straight into the bathrooms unhindered.

Those money people, Frau Bertram says, they don't have it too bad.

Well, you say, but you can see the sky from your apartment, beyond all those construction cranes.

Frau Bertram says a top-floor apartment in the building you're facing costs eight thousand euro a month in rent.

That can't be right, you say.

It is, Frau Bertram says, Frau Richter told me, she saw the ad.

You still don't believe her, but it's certainly the case that you and Frau Bertram are two of the few people still living in unrenovated apartments in your neighborhood. Below you, the concrete-slab construction of your building is falling apart. On the first floor, feces rise from the sewers into the tenants' bathtubs, and the wind presses through the warped window frames in all the apartments. You and all your neighbors know it's too late to move out, if you want to stay in the area and not be forced out to the edge of town.

But, you say—picking up the thread because you like stories told by people with no money about people who allegedly have a lot of money—I don't believe anyone would pay that much to live here. This isn't Munich or London.

Ach, says Frau Bertram, I don't know what this here is.

Frau Bertram's father waves from the balcony. He's a gray figure with dark circles beneath his eyes; his hearing's bad and he leaves the house once a day, walks once around the backyard doubled over, shakes his head over the children playing there, and goes back inside.

Gotta go, says Frau Bertram. She pauses as she leaves. I've got less time now. They put me on a work program. Housekeeping, she says. We clean the money people's homes and I'm hoping I'll get a job out of it; cross your fingers for me.

You're standing at the edge of the street, opposite the renovated building that people have been moving into for days even though work is still being done on the façade. Frau Bertram heads off and you go with her, walking her to the front entrance of your building.

Where is the work program? you ask her.

In the Waldstrasse neighborhood, says Frau Bertram, where the up-market people live.

They're not that up-market, you say.

Oh, they are, says Frau Bertram, or they act like it. She tells you she doesn't get paid for her work, she just cleans as part of the program and she's not allowed to leave even five minutes early, not even if she takes a shorter lunch break. And sometimes, she says, one of them wants his undershirts ironed, but when they're ironed they say it's not done right. Some people are never satisfied. While Frau Bertram looks for her keys in her handbag, you lean against the wall for a moment. The pebbles mixed in with

(206)

the concrete press against your back through your jacket. Maybe, you say, you're getting paid not so much for the housework and more so that someone has you to be dissatisfied with. Oh right, you say, because you've just remembered you don't get paid at all. Frau Bertram opens the door and walks inside; you follow her. A pebble has come loose from the wall and falls on the ground.

They really won't let us leave a minute earlier, Frau Bertram says.

Discipline, you say. Frau Bertram laughs. You climb the stairs, easily today, and think about what might be the appropriate reaction to Frau Bertram not getting paid, like some intern, and why someone doesn't want to let her leave early in the first place. You think it might be a good thing (or it would be something, at least, and something is definitely necessary, so it would be a good thing) if Frau Bertram were to knock pebbles out of the façade with a hammer and chisel. It would keep her busy for a long time and it would look good.

What can a person do who always has to work or to go to appointments at the welfare office, what can a person actually do, considering we all need money?

You remember an article about a woman who lived only by bartering, or in fact by being a barterer. She moved in with friends to help them, receiving food and clothing in return. The article made no mention of whether the friendship stood up to being expanded into a business relationship, or whether the friendship was overwritten by that business relationship. Everything the woman did seemed to have an exchange value that enabled the woman to make a living for herself. The woman apparently had to talk about everything, and she always had to establish whether she was there to work, whether her presence was already furnished with an exchange value or she was simply present for socializing reasons. How might those negotiations take place? Wouldn't they always have to establish whether the woman was already exchanging something? Wouldn't the person with her suddenly jump up to ask: Are you actually keeping me company for payment or are you just here for pleasure? Are you waiving your fee voluntarily because it's pleasant here or because nothing here is work for you? And might you suddenly change your mind? The article didn't mention any of that.

The woman's rebuke to all those who didn't endorse her life full of exchange value, all those who didn't barter, was: You're all children of capitalism and you can't turn down the hand that only apparently feeds you to go looking for new parents.

After reading the article you'd thought you ought to try it out too. Now, you see: the woman has perfected capitalism, has transported it willingly into the most private of sectors, has internalized it and is only under the impression that she's eliminated it.

You don't want reports on exotic antitheses to the world, you want theses with possibilities for living in this world. You want workers who are able to report on the conditions of their work, who don't have to defend themselves and every choice they've taken in their reports, but are clear enough to distinguish between who they are themselves and what conditions demand or seem to demand of them. You wish national newspapers would carry regular columns, glosses, and articles written by employees, and the employees would reap neither praise nor punishment from their commentaries. That it wouldn't be like this, for example:

> After joining Wal-Mart as a cashier in 1994, the first named plaintiff in the case, an African American woman named Betty Dukes, was demoted and subjected to other disciplinary actions for identifying discrimination through the company's "Open Door" hotline—a 1-800 number for internal complaints eventually known among Wal-Mart employees as "1-800-YOU'RE-FIRED."

Your outstanding invoices do get paid, incidentally, and your account even expands a little, for a while. It won't stay that way but that doesn't matter. You give up on your sense of urgency and the assumption that the future is being negotiated at every moment. You get new commissions, so you translate some things and you ask sometimes more, sometimes less for the work. The winter calms down, gives up on snow.

At the end of February, you get a phone call. An Amazon employee calls you to give you feedback. You're briefly tempted to simply hang up on him—you don't want any feedback—but your curiosity wins out.

We were very satisfied with your work, he says. Everything was more or less fine.

You say: Thanks, I'm glad to hear it. And you mean it too.

He says: Is there anything else I can do for you?

You say: I'd like to give Amazon some feedback too.

Oh, he says, OK.

You say: I didn't understand why different targets applied in the two types of shifts. And why the turbo shift gets to choose the products that are easiest to receive, so that the other shift only gets the leftovers—why that doesn't get changed even though everyone knows it.

Hmm, he says, struggling to find words that sound diplomatic. I would say that we are aware of the problem.

Aha, you say.

And we're dealing with it, he says.

That's good, you say.

Thanks for your feedback, he says, using your first name.

You're welcome, you say.

He says: Perhaps we'll have more work for you soon. Then he says goodbye.

You don't know exactly what that just was. You walk around your study and then go back to translating. You'll end up working on the translation until the early hours of the morning; it's due in three days' time. You feel free; you say it out loud over and over. With your slowly rising fees and your sprawling working hours that clutch at all times and all other activities, you haven't yet come to the following conclusion:

> The present performance subject is identical to the Hegelian slave apart from the circumstance that it does not work for the master, but exploits itself voluntarily. As an entrepreneur of itself, it is both master and slave simultaneously.

I wrote: We won't be leaving this book before you've taken action.

I'm not sure: Have you taken action or not?

Yes, you have.

We'll see.

Let's stay in touch.

Although you're not a futurologist, you can predict with almost 100 percent certainty what the company will do in the future. It's all clearly recognizable.

You read:

> Amazon is investing some 775 million dollars in buying a warehouse robot manufacturer. The US

company Kiva Systems specializes in technology designed for operating warehouses largely automatically. Amazon can make good use of that technology—millions of items have to be sorted and dispatched in its logistics centers.

The Kiva Systems robots are used by various large retailers. Founded 2003, the company is not listed on the stock exchanges. The takeover should be completed during the second quarter, according to an Amazon press release.

You knew all that long ago, and you don't have any objection.

In March, by which point you never think of your work at Amazon and can barely remember what it was like there and why the work troubled you so much, you receive a letter from Amazon. Next to your address, there's a small photo of part of the staff. Most of the employees are in the middle and the back of the blurry picture. The rows are looser in the foreground and at the edges. In front of the thick middle is a white banner that reads *amazon.de*. When you try to see who's holding the banner, you realize it's not a real banner, it's a layer of text inserted over the picture. Several employees in the front rows are raising their hands to wave.

Dear Ms …,
First of all we'd like to thank you once again for your hard work during the preholiday period.

Due to your excellent performance, we'd like to recommend you for further employment in our company.

Should you be interested in working for our company again this year, feel free to call us at any time.

Our Human Resources team will be happy to arrange a starting date with you.

With best wishes,

Your Human Resources Department

Amazon Distribution GmbH

You put the letter down on the pile of inbound bills that need filing away. Enough time appears to have passed, you note, for the company to start using your surname again.

I often feel privileged to have translated particular books, and this one is no exception. "Translation goes beyond reading," says Jhumpa Lahiri, "the act is visceral as opposed to merely intimate, and it impacts you, it teaches you in a different way." Translating this book, in which Heike Geissler has made me imagine and mentally re-perform the humiliation of working at Amazon, has hit me especially hard.

In *This Little Art*, Kate Briggs thinks about (among other fascinating things) the act of translation as writing, "conceived as a means of writing the other's work out with your own hands, in your own setting, your own time and in your own language with all the attention, thinking and searching, the testing and invention that the task requires." For me, translation is a way to claim another person's writing for myself, to immerse myself in it and, in mimicking it subjectively in my own language—what other way can there be?—to make my mark upon it.

This is a book about work, so I'd like to tell you a little about how Heike worked on it in the first place, and how I worked on its translation. Our work on the book was much more of a pleasure than Heike's time in the fulfillment center.

Heike got her job at the Amazon warehouse in Leipzig in 2010. Though the work was physically and mentally exhausting, she managed to take notes on Post-its while on the job, jotting down book titles or striking phrases, and she would write longer lists of what she had come across at home most evenings, in a diary-like format. Later, she wrote a factual report on her time at Amazon, but it was dull and dry and five publishers turned it down.

In 2013, Heike decided, "I'm going to rescue my book!" She restructured it entirely, changing the perspective as an experiment that gave her more control over her readers' interpretation, making it much more playful, adding less factual elements, and blending in events and ideas that came later. She decided to record an audio version chapter by chapter and put it on the Internet. It was emancipating, she felt, an act of reclaiming her rejected text through a noncommercial project, and she had a lot of fun reworking it all. I hope you can tell that by reading it. She started recording the chapters in her study at night, once the children were asleep.

After a couple of chapters had gone online, Mathias Zeiske from the literary magazine *EDIT* contacted Heike and asked whether they could publish two of them in written form. They did—and that was where I first came across it. They ended up publishing the whole thing as a book in a new series, Volte from Spector Books. At this point Heike took the audio off her website, because she did want to make a bit of money out of it if she could.

It was a good decision, she tells me. She's still being invited to interesting events to do with the book, four years after it came out in 2014. She wants to be read, and to be understood, not to be part of a literary scene or industry. She feels like a cowboy, she says, and both of us enjoy our roles on the margins of literature.

The translation came about in stages too. I was thrilled by the chapters I read in *EDIT*, and when the book came out I reviewed it and wrote that I'd love to translate it. Heike read the review and contacted me to say thanks. She's like that. When we eventually met up a few months later with Mathias, we agreed to try and get an extract published somewhere in English. Mathias knew someone who knew someone, and the first two chapters ended up in *n+1* in my translation.

Meanwhile, I tried pitching the book to US and UK publishers. I'm not sure why (I never am) but they weren't interested. Perhaps they didn't want to annoy Amazon, or perhaps it was hard to understand, without reading it, what makes the book so much more than an investigative account. Then the German writer and translator Kevin Vennemann recommended Heike Geissler to Semiotext(e), having himself translated Chris Kraus, an editor there, into German. I got an email asking if I'd translate the whole book, and I leapt at the chance.

But when I sat down to start the translation, I worried. I've had my fair share of shitty jobs but none of them were in a warehouse. Translating is often an act of empathy—

how would I put this in my language if I were to experience it? It helps to have experienced something similar. I found it difficult to imagine what the place looked like, how things worked, and I felt I needed to know that. Aside from that, the specific workplace has its own vocabulary, some of it in English even though the people inside the warehouse are German speakers—a kind of industrialized linguistic colonialism. In the maximally automated Amazon system, one size fits all; why use new terms just because the workers might not understand the usual ones? I know about this automated culture, to some extent, because I translated two of Amazon Crossing's very first titles, but I signed a nondisclosure agreement so I can't tell you anything about the process.

How could I find out that most basic of things: what *words* are used in other dispatch centers? I wanted readers who'd worked at Amazon themselves to recognize what was going on. Heike worked at the receiving end of the chain, unpacking boxes and entering products into the system. There have been a few undercover journalism pieces but the journalists went into far less detail, felt less a part of the system, and happened to work in different sections of the warehouses. It was then that I discovered YouTube as a research tool.

There are about five and a half million hits on YouTube for "Working at Amazon." I spent an afternoon in this rabbit hole, enchanted by so many different people talking to their webcams about their jobs. Some shared their insights as a kind of public service, giving tips to others who might want to work for the company. Some videos were parts of whole series based around individual lives, with dogs barking and moms barging in. One was by a young trans man, part of a diary-like project providing him with room for reflection and emotional support via the comments section; one was by a video gamer who usually talked about the latest releases. Several of them were followed up by "Why I Quit Working at Amazon" episodes. All of them talked about how boring the training day was. I loved every one of those people—and I was shocked all over again at how much they had to put up with. Eventually, the videos became repetitive; it seems Amazon really does do everything exactly the same way in every location.

For balance, I also watched a B2B video produced by Amazon itself, about how inventory is received into the system. That helped me to visualize the work process, and also amused me with the way its talk of "six-sided checks of each unit" contrasted with Heike's reality of cursory inspections under time pressure. As it turned out, real life also made adjustments to a few of the words used on the job, with the English job title "problem solver" reduced to the German "problemer," for example. Heike plays with these insidious euphemisms, the barefaced lies of "flat hierarchies" and "special handling." Hence the ugly title, SEASONAL ASSOCIATE, the word *associate* here so far removed from the idea of sharing and partnership that it makes me snort with cynical laughter.

I found that and other job titles on a web platform where people review employers they've worked for in the past. The logic of the Amazon review is something I actually admire in some ways—anyone can write one, it's democratic in that sense, yet it's hard to tell how far to trust an opinion. Here, that premise is turned on the company itself. From "stressful and downgrading workplace" to "Amazon is putting a smile on faces and changing the world," there are over twenty thousand reviews of various jobs at Amazon. Their overall average rating is 3.7 out of five stars. (The National Guard has a 4.5 average rating; Trader Joe's, 4.2; Penguin Random House, 4.1.)

So I had the language worked out after a while, but what about the cultural aspects? Part of the translator's job is to guess what her readers will and won't know about the foreign setting, how much help they'll need to understand, and how to give them that help. The gift that Heike's second-person perspective gave me, as her translator, was that it allowed me to add straightforward explanations of my own. She's already explaining how things are, so I could add extra layers where I thought it necessary. All I had to do was stay in line with Heike's style, continue my mimicry but this time imagine how Heike would have put it in the first place. It's not essential to the book as a whole that it's set in Leipzig—but there are parts that make more sense when we know that explicitly, and understand certain cultural traditions. And, as in most translations, there is wordplay that might otherwise be lost. Maybe this is the equivalent of explaining a punch line, but I hope my interjections work in the context.

This is where I have most clearly made my mark, I suppose, on Heike's text. Although I did ask her for permission, I haven't identified these additions; there are no footnotes or parentheses. That way, it feels to me like a synthesis of both our work. Heike and I have become friends in the course of all this—we have a lot in common. I hope reading our book is half as stimulating and thought provoking for you as translating it has been for me.

Afterword by Kevin Vennemann

Seasonal Associate—Labor and Self

in an Ocean of Time

Six, maybe seven minutes into *Meshes of the Afternoon* (1943), there is this short scene, really just a few takes: the film's lead character (director Maya Deren herself), swirling arms, dilated eyes, crawls across the living room ceiling of Deren's Spanish Colonial home at 1466 North Kings Road. Trying to break away, she keeps being pulled back, as though by magnetism, and then, from up there, she spots herself asleep in the living room armchair below, dreaming of herself being stuck, swirling arms, dilated eyes, on the living room ceiling of this same home in Hollywood, California. And so on. A few cuts later, by the arched living room window, Deren's character watches herself run up the driveway repeatedly in pursuit of a mirror-faced, cowled creature we just recently reencountered in a video by musician Janelle Monáe. Here, unfazed by the distance of seven decades, the ghoulish specter seems to be dancing with its manifestation from back when Deren was watching herself chasing it.

Running just under 15 minutes, *Meshes* is a deceptively short arrangement of complex depth, which challenges us to distinguish the main diegesis from the various interwoven dreams and visions to which Deren's character abandons herself. Which of the many identical women is the protagonist and which are mere apparitions? Is that her over there holding a knife, and which of the three Derens gathered around the dining room table is the real one, which are duplicates, and is it Deren's character herself who appears to be emerging from the ocean a giant?

Of all these many-layered, many-angled perspectives, the living-room-and-window scene has always stood out to me for its visualization of a twofold out-of-body experience Marx diagnosed as one of our fundamental, most devastating experiences in capitalism. (1) "Man," he writes, "duplicates himself not only, as in consciousness, intellectually, but also actively, in reality, and therefore he sees himself in a world that he has created."[1] Working, as we do, to reproduce and sustain ourselves, physically, intellectually, socially, we shape the world according to our needs, as has been our objective throughout Judeo-Christian civilization, and in this same creation, we see our reflection. Throughout *Meshes*, however, Deren seems so unsettled by her various other selves sleeping, dreaming, tossing and turning on ceilings, longingly standing by Spanish windows, running up driveways,

---

1. Karl Marx, *Economic and Philosophic Manuscripts of 1844*. Transl. by Martin Milligan (Prome-theus: Amherst, NY, 1988), 77.

chasing monsters that whatever it is she sees in these cinematic fragments of hers, it must be far more or far less than just her uncorrupted self-as-the-world. (2) Indeed, for Marx, too, our seamless reproduction is no less a dreamlike ideal than is the notion of complete *dominium terrae* without any loss. In capitalism, he notes, any encounter with ourselves outside ourselves is more likely due to our profound sense of alienation, one of the most pernicious outgrowths of the bourgeoisie glomming on to the means of production. Alienation does not imply two irreconcilably separate expressions of one and the same human incarnation. Instead, suddenly compelled to hawk our labor power to only the cheapest buyers on this new capitalist market, we are forced to distill ourselves and everything we are (our time, that is, all our energies and emotions, our public and private lives, even our political selves, our *being*) into the commodified reifications of our labor. From now on and until the revolution, our reflection assumes the shape of "the object which labor produces." It

> confronts [the producer] as *something alien*, as a *power independent* of the producer. [...] The alienation of the worker in his product means not only that his labor becomes an object, an *external* existence, but that it exists *outside him*, independently, as something alien to him, and that it becomes a power on its own confronting him; it means that the life which he has

conferred on the object confronts him as something hostile and alien.[2]

This object does not visually mirror us, of course. For the longest time, though, this short scene in *Meshes*—Deren on the ceiling, in her armchair, by the window, on the driveway—provided me with a helpful illustration, imperfect as it might have been, of what Marx was saying. And why not? Considering her socialist past and penchant for psychoanalysis, it made perfect sense to expect Deren to have searched for an adequate cinematic expression of the divide between herself as herself here and herself as an alienated specification of "man" over there. In 1943, after all, the revolution had not yet taken place, not really anyway.

* * *

Then, in 2014, when Heike Geissler published her novel, essay, maybe treatise, possibly meditation *Seasonal Associate* with Edition Volte/Spector Books in Leipzig, she provided me and us with at least as compelling a display of similar alienating processes. A literary sensation at the age of twenty-five, when her debut novel, *Rosa*, was published in German in 2002 to great critical acclaim, Geissler had to resort to odd jobs only a few years later when the infamous second-and-third-novel problem threatened to reduce her

2. Ibid., 71–72.

literary revenue to a trickle. *Seasonal Associate*, Geissler's account of one of these jobs, a grueling stint at an Amazon distribution center, has since rekindled her career as a writer, translator and rare political voice in German literary circles. Serendipitously, detailing an experience which had led her far outside herself seems to have allowed her to be again who she was supposed to be.

Some argue, as the later Marx certainly did, that there is no work or labor which could possibly be fulfilling; that even the idea of true self-actualization is an illusion; that we, as long as there is any need for either work or labor, are simply not ourselves, and we can never just *be*; that there is not even much difference between making a living by producing art and doing so by tending the conveyor belt, and that the former simply happens to be a more pleasant way to satisfy an unfortunate necessity. Geissler's narrator, on her addressee's behalf, thinks otherwise: "You prefer dealing with people who are what they do. A few years ago you were asked whether what you're looking for is authenticity. The question came from a slightly confused journalist, and you answered yes." (21) At least in part, the critical success of *Seasonal Associate* might have been due to the fact that Geissler has captured to such terrifying effect the utter human vacuity surrounding the de-authenticating epitome of division of labor, the conveyor belt. By so doing, she has touched on the most harrowing future scenario the majority of us, her lettered audience, are capable of entertaining. This is a scenario that prefigures the possibility, small as it might be, that we, too, could someday have to forfeit our questionable privilege of being "people who are what they do."

* * *

Geissler's premise is reminiscent of Deren's, but the armchair has been replaced with something much less comfortable: "You sit on the last free chair and breathe through your mouth" (17). Deren's duplicate dreams of other duplicates, while Geissler's narrator's "you" dreams of "fill[ing] up your account, which has reached the limits of its extendibility, and chang[ing] banks" (26). Already having lived through everything that is still ahead of her addressee, Geissler's narrator is blessed with the kind of creative control that Deren's character in *Meshes* does not get to exert over its various iterations. From safe enough a distance, recounting her story, recreating herself in that story, the I hovers high above this free chair as if pinned to the ceiling by the vigorous omniscience of first- *and* second-person narrative. From all the way up there, she gets to arrange her past self below within the plot: "You'd be sitting there, just like I sat there and just like you're now sitting there as me." (19) This is not the only time Geissler has her narrator expose the self-assured metafictionality of her storytelling: "We're not leaving this book until you've taken action." (170) Action, of course, the addressee will take— in fact, it is implied that after having passed through everything, she will assume narrative responsibilities, then proceed to write this very book about what by then will have become her own former self waiting on that only available chair in the hope of landing a job at Amazon. And so on.

In the English translation, the relative distance the narrator creates between herself and herself can only be much less emphatic than in the original. The German language has at its disposal not one, but two distinct ways of approaching the singular other, *Sie* and *du*. The former is the professional, respectful, at times submissive way to do so; the formal addressee usually owns the mandate to insist on being addressed as such. *Sie* is used in public settings to create and maintain the very distance between us and you that may be necessary for us to keep you at bay. More or less tacit social norms will enforce the correct utilization of *Sie* versus *du*. Violators are frowned upon or worse. *Du*, on the other hand, is typically employed among friends and family members. It engages children, adolescents and pets, but it also informs absent-minded soliloquy with ourselves, instances of road rage, anger in general toward anyone. Conveniently and quite intentionally, the *du* reduces the adult objects of our scorn to children, to adolescents or pets. Naively underestimating the formality of any given setting by using *du* is cringeworthy at best.[3]

---

3. This distinction applies to varying degrees to the different German-speaking countries, with Germany being the most formal, Switzerland the least. Using *du* to address your college professor in Germany would be considered insulting at the very least, whereas it is not uncommon in the same context in Switzerland. While Austrian urban centers generally tend toward the more formal, some Austrian rural areas emulate the Swiss model.

Retrieving herself from the past in this scene, placing herself into the narrative and onto that last free chair, Geissler's narrator uses *Sie* to address her former self: "Sie säßen da, genauso wie ich dasaß, und wie Sie als ich nun sitzen." / "You would be sitting there, just like I sat there and just like you're now sitting there as me," or, as Marx noted, "as *something alien*, as [the] *power independent* of the producer." The addressee shapeshifts into this power as soon as she morphs into an employee, that is, into both agent and product of her work. Writing and telling the addressee's subsequent fate (which is implied to be her own), the narrator gets to exert again the very control she relinquished the same moment she traded writing for toiling at Amazon—the moment her story became "*something alien*" from herself.

This formal distance is not fixed; it decreases, increases again, and the narrator, empowered by her storytelling, gets to design her conjured former self according to her preferences: "You, until I think otherwise, are courageous and strong, and I, until I think otherwise, am the opposite of you." (48) She supports her former self with recourse to her own experiences: "and there's something very old inside you, something that comes from me, which I hereby hand over to you so that you can deal with it, give it the full treatment and get it over and done with once and for all." (62) And every once in a while, she takes a break and briefly preoccupies herself with other things:

While you're working towards the end of your shift and you're tired and hungry [...], I'm sitting in a café in town with a friend. We're drinking white wine spritzers and chatting; we haven't seen each other for a while. [...] I come to collect you, still in a talking mood. I talk away at you, [...]. Over and over again. You don't really listen to me. (89–91)

Is the addressee not listening because she is upset about her narrator having left her alone for just a moment? A few encounters later, this reciprocally supportive yet fragile duality almost comes apart: "Knowing exactly how you feel, of course, I suppose I shouldn't be surprised; but I am. Why all these feelings of yours all of a sudden? You're nothing like this really." (151) All of a sudden, the narrator fails to comprehend her own former self.

Generally, though, she has firmly reestablished her alienated self as a reliable conversation partner to compensate for the humanity and maturity that corporate business philosophy so categorically denies her. Robert, the team leader, who keeps confusing brilliant leadership with threats of corporal punishment ("push-ups"), elaborates:

As you'll have noticed [, we only use *du* around here]. We're an international corporation but as you know our roots are in America. And Americans don't have a formal term of address like the German *Sie*, so we don't use it either. [We all use *du* around here,] from the bottom to the top, that's how it works here. (35)[4]

Far from being balanced or level, the resulting environment is hostile and destructive. Tact, deference, formality are vehemently proscribed, and casual brashness is purported to be a virtue, the great equalizer even: "Of course you know exactly where you are. You're in a so-called flat hierarchy, in which all flat hierarchists are gagging for an opponent." (171) Entirely bereft of its secondary functionalities as an indicator of warmth, family, friendship, proximity, the *du* has been reduced to its passive-aggressive and dehumanizing implications so that the addressee, at her lowest and most desperate, can think of no other way to stand up for herself than to insist on being addressed like all adults in Germany deserve to be. Toward the end of a nonsensical argument with an unnamed co-worker, the man says:

> Are you kidding me?
>
> You insist that he use *Sie* when talking to you, you] turn away and walk across the hall [...]. Your hands are trembling; you're ashamed of yourself. (103)

Shame. While the narrator's exclusive use of *Sie* with her former self enables her to distance herself from past events

---

4. For reasons of readability, the English translation of *Seasonal Associate* had to omit most passages discussing the conflict between using *Sie* and *du*. Whenever necessary, I have included some of these passages here and below in brackets.

that must be told even though they are painful to evoke, her main motivation is to assist her (and her*self*, retroactively) in easing the shame and self-loathing that come with the humiliation of being denied who we think we are or want to be. This is the kind of distance she creates between her selves, a distance of humanity-affirming formality.

* * *

Norman and Sandy, Heiner and Sebastian are the names of some of the addressee's superiors. Ironically, for a number of reasons too elaborate to discuss here, both Anglophone names indicate solid East German, pre-1989 biographies; "Heiner" suggests a man of advanced middle-age and "Sebastian" a man in his late thirties. All these people are adults with histories, experiences, emotional biographies, and, theoretically, the ability to exercise a certain restraint and even civility within social settings such as the workplace. Then there's Robert, the aforementioned "sports economist" and MBA student, charged with the difficult task of imparting to his underlings advanced American business ideals. He succeeds: there's even a gang of strikebreakers sporting T-Shirts with the unlikely slogan "*We love Amazon*" (120). Employed by a service industry, all these people and many more are, according to Marx's definition, workers. They all have in common, however, that they appear to identify with their exploiter, for whatever reason and to whatever end. This identification, coerced or not, has turned them from adults into repressed emotional cripples with little control over anything they say. Some of these people, we are inclined to polemicize, have been brainwashed, while others might have cultivated a frightening assiduousness consonant with their individual nature, and they just happen to be working for Amazon. Others still might have no choice but to play along. Anyone who has ever worked away from the consuming solitude of their own desk at home will have encountered some of these types and likely many others. Marx: "The estrangement of man, and in fact every relationship in which man stands to himself, is first realized and expressed in the relationship in which a man stands to other men."[5] When a person is incapable of overcoming their own discomfort at not being anything resembling themselves, chances are they cannot help exposing those around them to the incurable, violent lack within themselves. It is the weight of social alienation borne by all these people in equal measure that, in Geissler's novel, hits the addressee with full force when she realizes the necessity to relinquish even the slightest hope that something as fundamental as *language* could still be worth anything in this environment. "Good grief, you think, surely it's not that difficult to say something normal." (179) But it is. Whatever it is the narrator first perceives as new, then as irritating, then

5. Marx, *Manuscripts*, 79. For the purposes of this paper, I have ignored the subtle and complicated differences between Marx's usage of *alienation* versus *estrangement*.

as infuriating—it has long been the actual, the new "normal" here:

> In the midst of the other newbies, you're in an unknown land with an unknown language and the person who's supposed to show you everything doesn't understand what a stranger doesn't know or can't know and what has to be explained to you. Norman says: You don't have to understand it, by the way, you just have to know it. (70)

This is normal now: the corrosion of sincerity, the individual's utter inability and/or refusal to act and listen and engage empathetically with anyone and for any reason. As soon as the addressee has passed through the distribution center's well-protected gates, any effort at any meaningful exchange will always already have been thwarted. "Hence within the relationship of estranged labor each man views the other in accordance with the standard and the relationship in which he finds himself as a worker,"[6] and everyone in his vicinity turns into an enemy to the same extent that his own, alienated self has become one. A hostile object. It is Geissler's immeasurable accomplishment to have rendered so tangible the gradual yet relentless disintegration of language when nothing anyone says is ever really expected to matter anymore—not even among

6. Ibid., 79.

adults. *Seasonal Associate* systematically catalogues what little is left of language and just about everything that has contributed to its destruction. It is a truly depressing portfolio, showcasing the astounding richness of our passive aggressions and a wealth of truculent personal interactions. There is the verbal residue of suppressed and/or disappointed ambition, for instance. There is

- the ubiquitous tendency to "talk to [others] like I sometimes talk to my children" ("She yells: How often do I have to tell you that!" (49));
- the incessant, pseudo-humorous belittlement, riddled with insecurity and self-disdain, of anyone who could be more powerful in real life ("Little Miss Professor, he says, you go ahead and take them all out if you like." (70));
- a host of casually violent threats, sallies of inhumanity ("She shouts: One of these days I'll end up killing one of you" (84)), as if anyone could possibly care this much about random co-workers arriving too early or too late;
- casual misogyny, again in the guise of the worst kind of humor, the "just kidding" kind ("Five days ago, he says, and now you're sending me this skinny little chicken. […] You're not as weak as you look, Heiner says." (144));
- exaggerated incredulity, fake exasperation ("It all has to get better. You're not new here anymore, honey" (176); "Four lamps per crate, four crates per pallet. Are you new here?" (194)), as if there were no other conceivable way to communicate perceived productivity deficiencies;

- the linguistically desperate escape into empty catchphrases ("Why make it simple when you can make it complicated? says the forklift guy." (195));
- and then there's…I don't even know what this is: "Hey, says Robert, remember the push-ups. […] If no one says anything we'll be sitting here till midnight, and I don't know about you but I've got better things to do." (36)

All these verbal atrocities are committed by the addressee's superiors—by adults, mind you. They exhibit the miserable state of a language informed and fostered by a destructive work environment that stifles even the tiniest sparks of solidarity.[7] The narrator calls it "employee language," predicting that she herself will inevitably fall prey to it: "You won't talk the way you normally talk" (57). She is wrong here, though. Instead giving up on herself, she diagnoses the even more sobering extent to which this anti-language of perennial spite has long since bled into everyday life:

> The old woman stands up and opens a window. A young woman is sitting next to the window. […] The woman in the anorak begins to murmur, complaining quietly but clearly about the older woman. […] It's

7. Marx did not foresee this venomous potential of language when he expressed his optimistic belief that, while capitalism deprived the individual artisan of just about everything, it also provided the emerging working class with everything it needed to unify and revolt. See Karl Marx, Friedrich Engels, *The Communist Manifesto* (London, New York: Penguin, 1991), 229–230.

ridiculous, says the man she's with. He gets up and slams the window shut. The old woman shakes her head, now murmuring herself. This, you think, is how wars are started[.] (119)

* * *

An ocean of time. Halfway into *Seasonal Associate*, the now-desperate addressee is still sitting, or sitting again, on that last free chair or an analogue thereof, it doesn't seem to matter, and nothing is likely to ever really matter again. "You close your eyes and sit in an ocean of time, as though you'd been working at Amazon for years […]. Your internal screenwriter demands a big closing scene, but none comes and it never will. Only thoughts, which go far but not far enough" (121), until they do go far enough after all.

At the very end of *Meshes*, Maya Deren's character loses herself in dreams about herself not *in* but *as* the ocean. Upon returning home, Alexander Hammid finds her in the living room armchair covered in blood and kelp as if there was truth to her dream, and indeed the entire mise-en-scène suggests this oceanic identity of hers. Romain Rolland, in a letter to Freud, described a similar experience as causing a feeling of liberation, "a sensation of 'eternity', a feeling as of something limitless, unbounded—as it were, 'oceanic.'"[8] In

8. Sigmund Freud, *Civilization and Its Discontents*. Transl. by James Strachey (New York: Norton, 1961), 11.

his response, Freud vigorously dismisses the deceptive appearance "of being one with the external world as a whole." Instead, he argues, the notion of "oceanic feeling" is valid only insofar as "the ego is continued inwards, without any sharp delimitation, into an unconscious mental entity which we designate as the id [...]. But towards the outside, at any rate, the ego seems to maintain clear and sharp lines of demarcation."[9] For Freud, the individual may gain an awareness of these lines of demarcation only by way of a confrontation with itself.

Seasonal Association is this very confrontation. How can we know if it succeeded? We cannot. Not even the narrator herself seems to be sure:

> I wrote: We won't be leaving this book before you've taken action.
> I'm not sure: Have you taken action or not?
> Yes, you have.
> We'll see. (211)

To which actions might she be referring? Maybe to the addressee's repeated, stubborn insistence on drawing similar demarcation lines in various conflicts with other employees; maybe to the very confrontation the narrator herself initiated by facing her past in the first place, by telling her story about her former self's return to herself.

9. Ibid., 12–13.

This action might have been one or all of the other redemptive developments just before the end: For purposes of rationalization and support, the addressee establishes a theoretical framework for her own and similar situations (the dialectics of master and slave, 209). She succeeds in forcing an Amazon representative to admit a major flaw in the company's approach to evaluating and compensating the various performance coefficients applied (210). Due to increased demand, she gets to raise her translation fees (209), thereby at least temporarily diminishing the profound feeling of "failure when you can't live off your actual job" (15) diagnosed at the outset. Whichever one of these actions is the one receiving credit here, all that matters is that both selves have survived; that they found themselves and each other, and while they might never be fully one again, they do have a plan: "Let's stay in touch." (211)

ABOUT THE AUTHOR

Heike Geissler's first novel *Rosa* received the Alfred Doblin Prize for debut fiction in 2002. She subsequently published the novella *Nichts was tragisch wäre*, in 2009, and a children's book in 2010. Her critically acclaimed nonfiction novel *Seasonal Associate* was published in Germany in 2015. Geissler received a fellowship fro the German Academy Rome Villa Massimo in 2017. She lives in Leipzig, where she teaches creative writing